inspiration sandwich
SARK'S JOURNAL and PLAY! BOOK
ADDRESS BOOK
LIVING JUICY
THE MAGIC COTTAGE
A creative COMPANION
THESE ARE THE OTHER BOOKS BY SARK

Succulent
Wild
Woman
Dancing with Your Wonder-Full Self!
By SARK
A Fireside Book
Published by Simon & Schuster

Brigette Scheel is The Book Production Manager we need her and Jupiter loves her ♥

Fireside
Rockefeller Center
1230 Ave of the Americas
New York
New York

This Book is Dedicated to:
Craig McNair Wilson
The Most Wild Man
Succulent I Know! ♥

Created by SARK

Manufactured and printed
in our United States of America!
10 9

Library of Congress
Cataloging-in-Publication Data
is Available CIP: 97-65622

ISBN
0.684.83376.X

Photo by Bruce Klemens page 158
Thank you to Cherlynne Li
Art Director!

Succulent:

ripe. juicy. whole.
round. exuberant. wild.
rich. wide. deep. firm.
rare. female.

Your Succulent

Being and Becoming A Succulent Wild Woman

Blocks to Succulence

Fears

Healing

Outrageous Adventures

Sexuality

books, resources

Menu Selections

Special note: you have permission to read in any order, no order, backwards or upside down as you wish

and MUSIC at the end of each chapter

Being A Succulent

- BATHE naked BY MOONLIGHT
- Marry your self first promise to never leave YOU
- Buy yourself Gorgeous Flowers
- Practice extravagant LOUNGING
- invent your Life over if it Doesn't feel JUICY
- Cradle your wounded places like precious BABIES
- Be Delicious
- eat mangoes naked lick the juice off your arms
- Discover your own Goodness
- Smile when YOU feel like it
- SHOUT: I'M Here! I'M succulent and I'M LOUD!
- Be rare eccentric and original
- Describe yourself as Marvelous

WILD WOMAN BY SARK

paint your SOUL

investigate your DARK places with a FLASHLIGHT

MAKE More Mistakes!

weave your Life into A net of Love

you Are enough
you HAVe enough
you Do enough

celebrate your Gorgeous Friendships with women

tell the Truth Faster

end Blaming

Dress to Please your Self

let your creative spirit rush. flow. tumble. leak spring. bubble stream. dribble out of you

Be inwardly outrageous

seek out other succulent wild women
en.courage the sharing of mutual treasures

THIS is A BOOK ABOUT celebrating being A succulent WILD WOMAN.

It Means Living Fully, richly, rarely and reveling in ordinary and extraordinary moments.

it Gives you permission, and calls you out to play!

I Believe we must live untamed, juicy and abundantly as women.

If we share our stories, we will have many telepathic companions for the journey.

We Are All riding creative cycles!
JUST WATCH US ride!

My own journey is full of fear, pain, love, shame, wonder, ecstasy, luck, daring, and marvelous imperfections.

I invite you to travel along with me as I share my stumblings, astonishments, and discoveries as a woman.

Whenever I read travel books, I am so grateful that other people go to far-flung places, climb mountains, join expeditions, and then write about their experiences. I feel grateful because I can vicariously travel with them

Without having to get out of bed!

we love to
STAY in BED...
our dreams will lead us to succulent places!

Here are some scenarios to go along with reading this book:

- in A SHAFT of SUNLIGHT, BESIDE A BOWL of oranges, BAREFOOT.
- in the BATHTUB with many candles and slices of mango.
- in WHITE cotton PAJAMAS, under A COMFORTER with A CAT sleeping in A circle.

I write All my BOOKS Lying DOWN in PAJAMAS and MEASURE time BY MUGS of tea.

remember PAJAMAS with feet? The feet HAD little white BUMPS that gripped onto everything

MY LUCKY POLKA DOT MUG

I do not know more than you do.
My investigations have shown that we frequently think others know [it] but we don't know [it].

What is [it]?

My younger brother, Andrew, always says,

"When you give these talks in public, be sure to start by telling people how many problems you have."

"Isn't it obvious?" I always think. Andrew says it's not. I guess I look bright and untroubled, and I smile a lot, which is sometimes a mask to hide shyness, fear, or pain.

The books I write have colorful, happy covers, which can cause people to think:

it Must Be easy For Her

It isn't easy for any of us to transcend the past, or pain we might have suffered. Yet, there are gifts in those pains, and we can choose to let light into the dark places. We are not alone!

"I have woven a parachute out of everything broken."

William Stafford

I was physically and sexually abused by an older brother for about 7 years. This caused me to live in my imagination and to create worlds other than the one I was actually living in.

This also set up patterns of self-destruction that became addictions and self-hatred that persisted for many years.

I've written about the incest in my second book: <u>Inspiration Sandwich</u> in a chapter called "Transforming Negatives."

I emerged from that incest to live a frantic and unconscious life, traveling and living with millionaires on tropical islands, and being described as "The Marshmallow Venus."

I often thought that if men could walk around in the world for one day as women, and hear the comments from other men that women hear, they would rush to us in incredulous disbelief, and help us to form safety patrols.

I spent many years being furious with men. I didn't realize that they were experiencing oppression of a different kind. I had to have an enemy, a place to rage. I had many examples of "bad men."

I didn't understand that my own self-hatred was being projected onto the world, and how much I was playing the part of the angry victim—and sometimes still am.

Now, I'm surrounded by marvelous men.

After many years of self-healing, therapy, and investigating my interior, I bring you this collection of stories, memories, simple truths, and succulence.

Succulent Wild Woman:

A woman of any age who feels free to <u>fully</u> express herself in <u>every</u> dimension of her life.

A note to young or not yet formed Succulent Wild Women:

Stand firm and whole as a woman. You are precious and irreplaceable. Treasure your female self. Choose innocence. Invent ways to feel more free. Investigate your darknesses.

A note to those who love Succulent Wild Women:

Learn thoroughly your own female side. Support freedom and release judgments. Be sexual only mutually. Let go of fears. Speak respectfully. Spend real, intimate time with women.

Invest in Succulence

CHOOSING SUCCULENCE

I am not always a positive person. People call my inspiration phone line, or read my books, and decide that I'm this super-positive person with glitter in her hair and a beatific smile (well, sometimes it's true...). . . . Glitter does seem to follow me . . .

Being "positive" is a choice. I am flooded with the same doubts, terrors, insecurities, rages, incessant worries, and critical inner voices as everyone else—maybe more!

Sometimes I go overboard describing my faults or flaws, to the extent that I see people cringe and wonder, "Why am I listening to/reading this person if she is so riddled with stuff?" We are all riddled with stuff!

I said this same thing to my therapist when I stopped idealizing him so much and saw his flaws. "You mean I'm just seeing a regular guy?" Or, as Elisabeth Kübler Ross says, "I'm not O.K., you're not O.K., and that's O.K.!" My positive self developed partly in response to the ugliness of the alternative. Some days, I feel myself sliding into a negative pool...

My friend Brigette calls this the "sea of bitterness"

Sometimes I just sit in a negative pool of my own making

Friends pull me out, or I catch myself.

In what ways are you tempted to collapse into the negative?

I feel it's much more interesting to focus on and magnify the postive. You can use a magnifying glass.

The negative is still there—it's just that the spotlight is on the positive.

Many of us grew up with a large focus on the negative. Part of this was generational, or just habitual. Phrases like, "Just wait until the other shoe drops."

poor dropped shoe

"Don't count your chickens before they're hatched."

1
2
3

"I'll give you something to cry about." "We didn't want you to get a swelled (or big) head."

Do you actually know *anyone* who got a "swelled head" from too much praise? Usually, it was far too little, and they retreated to their ego for escape and became grandiose as a type of defense. No matter how dry and scared we might be, I believe we must

CHOOSE SUCCULENCE

Succulence next stop

over and over. Sometimes hundreds of times in a day—or thousands!

The negative can be so seductive. You can usually find someone to spend time being critical, judgmental, and dark with.

Dark glasses

Complainers always find each other, and usually in some situation they've created to complain about! (note: As a "master complainer" myself, I'm working on the patterns that make this feel rewarding.) Being positive does not mean being accepting of the negative, or ignorant of the issues, or the world situation, or anything else.

It means seeing the grace in as much as you can see.

Like cloud watching... the shapes we see are created by our vision

Choosing succulence will enable us to be more alive, more contributing, flexible, and fresh. I ask myself frequently, "How can I turn this around? How can I see with succulent eyes?" Almost any situation can be seen in a new light.

A brand new light

"Tell all the truth—but tell it slant."

Emily Dickinson

Reprinted with permission of the publishers and Trustees of Amherst College from The Poems of Emily Dickinson, Thomas H. Johnson, ed., Cambridge, Mass.: The Belknap Press of Harvard University Press, Copyright © 1951, 1955, 1979, 1983 by the President and Fellows of Harvard College.

Choosing succulence is a deliberate act of personal revolution. It means waking up! Embracing your true self, studying your patterns, and letting out your most alive self. We all have one.

The succulent person is bursting with juices, stories, animations, ideas, and love. The dry person looks sideways and says, "Who do you think you are?"

Use an umbrella to shield yourself from this person

"If you asked me what I came into this world to do, I will tell you. I came to live out loud."

Emile Zola

Living A Wonder-Full Wild Life right now

wildness is like ivy growing through All our cracks

We Deserve wildness. Wildness can be as simple as wearing tall boots when none of your friends do, or talking to gorgeous strangers, or visiting expensive Hotels for just a cup of tea. Whatever takes us out of our routine and gives us a little interior spark, is wild.

Being tame is what we're taught.
. . . put the crayons back, stay in line, Don't talk too loud, Keep your knees together, nice Girls Don't . . .

As you might know, nice girls do, and they like to feel wild and alive. Being tame feels safe, Being wild, unsafe. Yet safety is an illusion anyway.

we are not in control.

As a controlling type of person, I hate this fact.

No matter how dry and tame and nice we live, we will Die. We will also suffer along the way.

Living wild is its own reward. Tiny wildnesses are everywhere to experiment with:

CRAYOLA

Throwing all of the crayons out of the box into a big wild color pile

Don't stand in line at the bank. Sit down and read a book. Put change into pay phones in the coin return.

The change will come back to you in another form

Sit with your legs up on the furniture and draw inside your own books.

When my boyfriend first read my books, he went through and wrote to me in all the spaces and margins. I treasure his murmurings.

Go wandering! Let the world show you the most wild path. Speaking to strangers is an excellent exercise. Use your intuition as guidance and <u>listen</u> to what you hear. Be exposed.

Live a wild, vulnerable life. Let us see you, laughing loudly, walking flamboyantly, and wearing colors that don't match.

My mother used to say that my sense of color was garish — look at me now, Mom!

Dress like an angel and walk a tight rope

Let us see you celebrating in public, eating heartily, creating boldly, dancing wildly or badly.

Sometimes I see women who look like captives. Dry and hunted, they scurry from curb to car. They look too thin and not joy-full. They don't go out unless it's with a man, or to the "right event."

Like blades, they are sharp and can be dangerous

Go out wildly and Alone

or with a selection of outrageous women friends

Go out in all your own wild glory

Living wild has consequences. Welcome these and learn from them. Please give yourself too many gifts! So often, I meet women who say, "I really shouldn't be buying all this for myself..." Why not? Don't you deserve it? My mother taught me not to wait for a man to buy me flowers. She always said, "Buy your own flowers, too."

and so I do...
I also receive them

Stop apologizing and saying, "I'm sorry" so much. Women have a terrible habit of apologizing for everything (even their own existence). One time, I bumped into a woman—hard—and she said automatically, "I'm sorry." I had bumped into her! Sorry in the dictionary says this: wretched, miserable, inferior in worth or quality. We are not this!

We have a right to live wild, succulent lives. right now. Open your window and yell at the top of your lungs:

"I'm here! I'm wild! I will live a daring and remarkable life!"

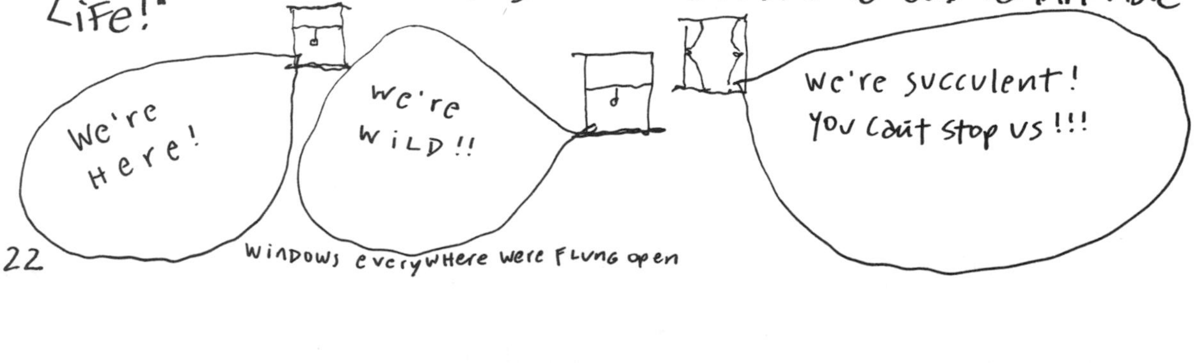
We're Here!
We're WILD!!
We're succulent! You can't stop us!!!

windows everywhere were flung open

WAKING UP
(and then, taking a nap)

It is tempting to sleepwalk through life. To tell half-truths, listen half-way, be half-asleep, drive with half attention...

WAKE UP!

We need you as an alive and awake woman, listening and contributing. Wake up your creative genius and let it out into the world. Wake up your power and use it wisely. Wake up to your pain and investigate it.

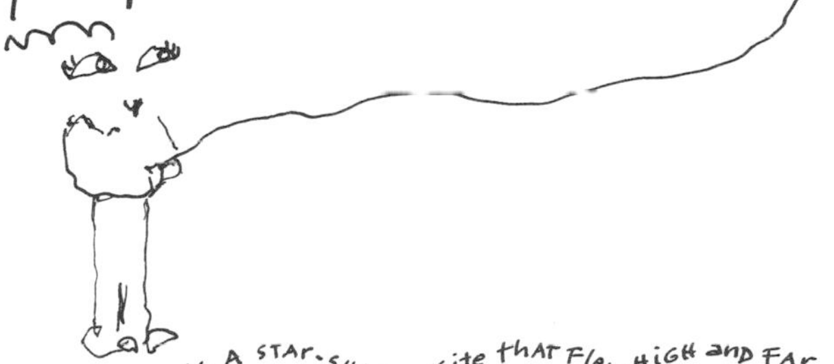

Her creative genius was a star-shaped kite that flew high and far

Wake up the dull old parts that are hiding from the light. Wake up to love and let it flood through you.

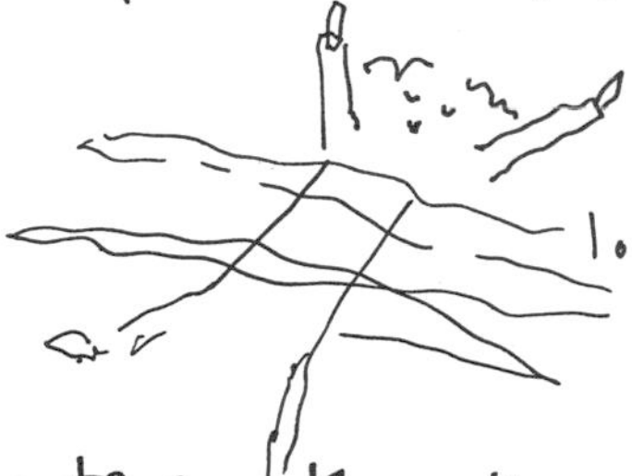

love flooded in and out

Wake up to see the other souls around you. Let them affect you. Live in the center of your life.

"Cluster together like stars."

Henry Miller

now that you've awakened...

immediately take a nap! Naps are when the angels come out to take special care of you.

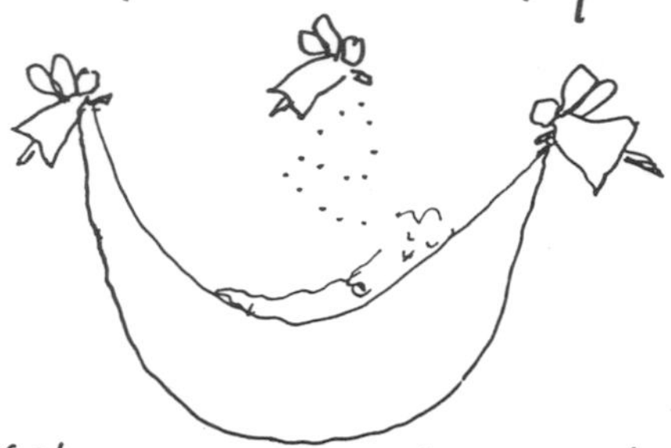

The angels carried her in a healing hammock and sprinkled dream dust on her

None of us get enough naps. Naps are essential for mental health. Naps *are* productive—contrary to what we've been taught.

The more naps you take, the more money you'll make! it's true.

Our culture promotes tension and crabbiness. Part of this is the severe lack of naps. Declare your home, or wherever you are, as a **Free nap zone.**

I met a woman in her 70's who came up to me after a workshop and said, "Thank you for giving me permission. My back is killing me. I'm going up to my hotel room and taking a nap! I have never done anything so self-indulgent. Isn't that sad?"

permission
permission
permission

plant and fly permission flags all over your life!

I dreamed the other night of music boxes hidden all over my garden. I think of us all as music boxes—beautiful and full of music... especially when we open up!

Being and Becoming A Succulent Wild Woman

Live the Life you Love
By Barbara Sher
The essential rumi
By Coleman Barks
There is nothing wrong with you
By Cheri Huber
Conscious Femininity
By Marion Woodman
Glimpses of Grace
By Madeleine L'engle
Wherever you go, There you are
By Jon Kabat-zinn
Fearless Creating
By eric Maisel Ph.D
nothing But the Marvelous
By Henry Miller
Hymn to an unknown God
By Sam Keen
Motherpeace Tarot
By Vicki noble
inspiration sandwich
By SARK
You Are the World
By Krishnamurti
Open Mind
By Diane Marie Child
Growing Season
By Arlene Bernstein
notes from my inner child
By Tanha Luvaas
How to Draw A radish
By Joy Sikorski

resources

- Barbara Sher Audio tape program, "Dare to Live your Dream." This Audio Tape series will show you How to Free your Gifts and create A Life you will love. To order, call 800·321·WISH

Music

- The yearning, romances for Alto Flute, By Michael Hoppé & Tim Wheater

Ramblings of a Dry and Tame Woman

I'm under "House Arrest." I put myself in this state so that I would actually write something instead of distracting myself in countless ways. I'm feeling very spoiled and self-indulgent and stupid. I keep eating things that make me sick. I keep thinking that I'll turn into some kind of "moderate person" who can have a box of thin mint Girl Scout cookies for longer than a day.

THin Mints
refrigerate For Best Taste...

visions of thin Mints danced in Her Head

I start out with 2 or 3 cookies in a bowl (imagining that I'm a "moderate person.") Then, it turns into 3 cookies every ½ hour until they're gone! The only way I can really resist is not to have them in the house at all—which gets scary when someone gives me a gift of a whole box of cookies (but thank you Angela!).

I'm learning to say "No thank you!" But sometimes I feel weak or old, or in need of some vital comfort that I haven't yet learned how to find inside myself.

During these times, I'm still learning to give myself love and self-acceptance. Admitting these things in writing helps. Learning that I'm not alone really helps.

Before I can really <u>live</u> as a succulent wild woman, I find that I must explore the dry, tame, dark parts of myself.

if she got really quiet and listened, new parts of her wanted to speak.

I resist my dark places, and try to hide them from other people, but mostly myself. Sometimes I just skip from one addictive behavior to another—whatever is loudest, and will most quickly fill the emptiness.

the Hole you can never Fill

How deep is the emptiness? even if you could manage to fill it, would that make you happy?

Sometimes I am able to meditate and go for a long nourishing walk. Sometimes I just lie flat and still in a darkened room, fumbling for the leg of God to hold onto.

Did you ever wonder what the leg of God would look like?

One of the ways to arrive at succulence and wildness is to allow the parts that aren't. I will list some of my faults and weaknesses in the hopes that it might inspire you to do the same. Letting it be seen takes away its power.

I'm codependent, a recovering incest survivor and almost an alcoholic (AAA!), obsessively/compulsively driven, overly sensitive and highly sensitive, subject to paranoid thinking and martyrdom, and I live largely in a state of denial. My therapist might add: narcissistically wounded.

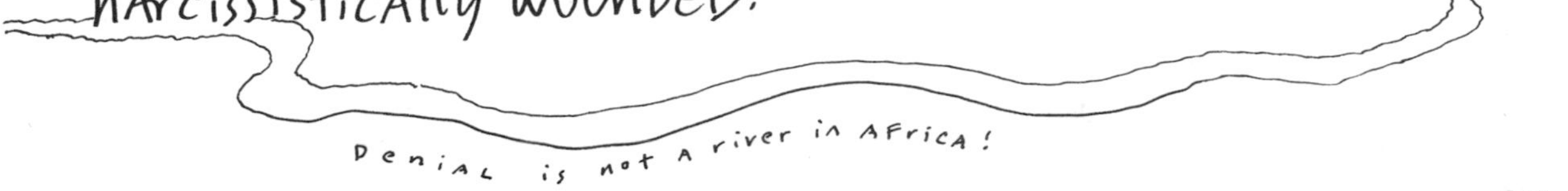
Denial is not a river in Africa!

If and when I think of other things to admit, you'll be the second to know.

I'm also very gifted, a good friend, occasionally wise, irreverent, rather extravagant, curious, outspoken, opinionated, quite brave, very flexible, power-full, and live mostly in my sense of humor.

I am a seeker, a believer and a creative being.

My furniture is all white. I drink only red wine. This makes me some kind of optimist.

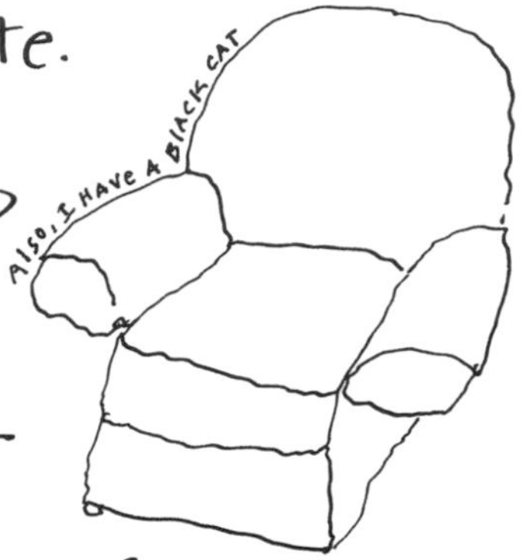
Also, I have a black cat

it was my first real furniture and I still get nervous that I can't just pack up all my stuff in a car anymore. I'd have to get movers—does this make me grown-up?

I'm stubborn, trusting, sarcastic, and an introvert who's learned extrovert skills. I avoid most forms of conflict and tremble at expressing an "unpopular" opinion.

Once we've rambled through our dry and tame places, we can begin to explore succulence. Succulent Wild Woman is a process, and an adventure. To discover, and recover, your own succulence is a voyage of the interior and exterior. Succulence comes from your center—the sweet, true part of you—your essence—that belongs to no one else.

Wildness is relative. Wild is a state of mind that relates directly to succulence. We are each in a process of being and becoming a

Succulent Wild Woman!

I am sharing my own journey so that you can be a part of my exploration.

I am very real—deeply human, partly human, splendidly and horribly imperfect, bent, disguised, loud, ever-changing, thought-full and thought-less, wildly narcissistic in certain spots.

How are you most human? What would a map of you look like? There are so many ways to be named and defined, yet we are ultimately a mystery. What a glorious thing!

I'm an Aries with Virgo rising and a Scorpio moon, a 9 on the enneagram, a sage in the Michael teachings, a secret and skeptical Christian, a dabbling Buddhist, and in a committed and monogamous relationship with a man.

We are all complex, imperfect human beans.

little beans, just bouncing along

I am particularly interested in women, and lovers of women. When I started writing this book, I was worried that men might feel left out.

Then, I recall hearing Maya Angelou recite her magnificent poem, "Phenomenal Woman," at Herbst Theatre in San Francisco. She said,

"Before I read this poem, I just need to say that I know there are a lot of incredible men out there, and that this poem may seem to exclude them—it doesn't. And I want to say to all the men out there, Honey—you got to write your own poems!"

write your lives so that others may be illuminated

How we stop ourselves

I am always "turning away from the ecstasy." There are things I know I love doing, yet I stop. Why?

Everytime I meditate, there is a benefit. Still, I stop myself all the time from doing it. My mind is filled with fresh and realistic reasons about "why it's not time to meditate." Exercise creates more oxygen and a "new mind," but I am almost frantic to postpone it. Eating well provides an almost instant reward. Yet I run to empty foods from childhood that used to comfort me, and now are sedating.

I'm often seduced by struggle.

It's as though it's painful to feel "too good." I'm used to the effort, and sometimes confused by the joy.

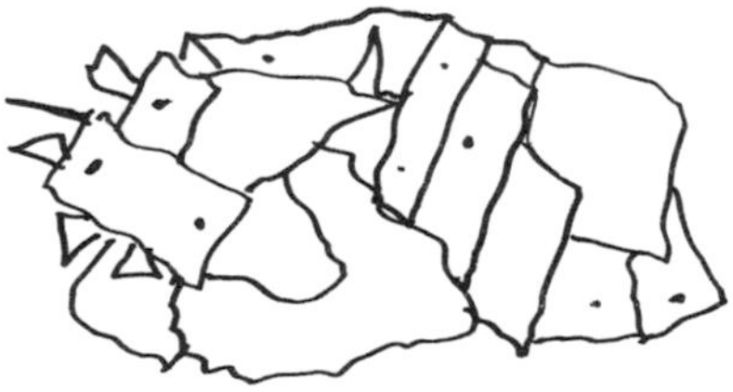
The structure of struggle
was made up of junk and fear

I am familiar with rejecting pleasure, and with a low-grade, almost constant feeling of despair. There are many companions for this journey, even though it makes no sense, I find myself clinging to sadness to avoid feeling my emptiness, or even happiness!

Sadness was slippery and kept changing shape
it wasn't nourishing
She tried clinging to the sadness
even though it repetitively hurt her

I think it is easy to stop ourselves from being too bright, too happy, too successful.

Conformity also soothes us. We can predict it, and there is the illusion of control.

Unfortunately, we also stop ourselves from being too visible, unusual or vivid.

"I am not eccentric! It's just that I am more alive than most people. I am an unpopular electric eel, set in a pond of goldfish!"

Dame Edith Sitwell

We stop ourselves from being too loud, too different, or too much.

Yet we crave our individuality, our wild, special selves. We want to live our adventures and be seen for our essences.

Who are you after the guests have gone home? Who are you after you take your makeup and clothes off? What do you dream about? Who are you reading? How do you stop yourself? Who are you?

ways you stop yourself:

Working with the Hard Parts

I am often running from pain

My tracks could be seen in the snow

When I feel helpless or out of control, I want to close up. Wall off. Medicate. The ego maniacally says No! to everything. I listen to it, and isolate to try to avoid the pain.

Pain arrows arrive silently and sometimes with no warning

She found a cave where she thought pain couldn't find her

Even the idea of pain: possible pain, invented pain, perceived pain, imagined pain, future pain, and, especially, present pain.

If pain seeps in, I seal off the entrances with some kind of barrier: distraction, food, sleep, bad TV movies . . . yet pain continues to seep until it bursts in, in some unguarded entrance, and catches me sleeping at 5 A.M., and I awaken sobbing.

"When something within us is disowned, that which is disowned, wreaks havoc."

Ralph H. Blum & Susan Loughan, The Healing Runes

It is clear that breathing into the pain works with body massage. Perhaps it also works with emotional pain. Turning toward a large wave in the ocean is the best defense. Diving into the huge wave can save you.

We must work *with* the parts that hurt

If there is darkness, we have our flashlights. If there is terror, we have our God. If there is despair, fear, anxiety, anger, or agony, we can become our own best parent and hold the little child inside of us.

This tiny child is waiting for comfort from you

"When you come to the edge of all the light you have, and must take a step into the darkness of the unknown, believe that one of two things will happen to you: either there will be something solid for you to stand on, or, you will be taught how to fly."

Patrick Overton

How can we be open to the hard parts and still function? Oh no! not **THIS** we say. Whatever **THIS** might be: an incapacity, a weakness, a cruel thought, a death, a misunderstanding, a joy not shared, a wistful, lonely moment.

THIS must be our greatest teacher.

Note: read the poem: "The Guesthouse" by Rumi

I myself still fight with almost every **THIS** that comes my way.

Working *with* the hard parts and not against them will create movement.

Investigating the Darkness

with a flashlight

A woman called my inspiration phone line and said, "I feel inspired by you because you are still investigating your dark sides— this gives me hope."

I used to avoid the darkness, the shadows, as much as possible because I mortally feared what might be hidden in there.

Then I was propelled into the darkness by memories of incest, self-destructive behavior, and other traumas.

shine your light into the dark spots

My therapist speaks beautifully about the darkness in a poem he wrote called, "The Museum of the Lord of Shame." This is an excerpt from his forthcoming poetry collection.

CODA

When you are small there is no protection
from shame
& now that you are older
your attempts to keep the unsafe out
costs you more than you can imagine
We need to breathe in the direction of danger...
& to sing
we must not only be wounded
-- for surely all of us are that
but be willing to suffer
the terrifying healing,
with its stations of humiliation,
shame, endurance & grief
-- Gary Rosenthal

The good news is that blocking the darkness also blocks the joy, and the succulence.

When we can face the dark, we will be flooded by the light.

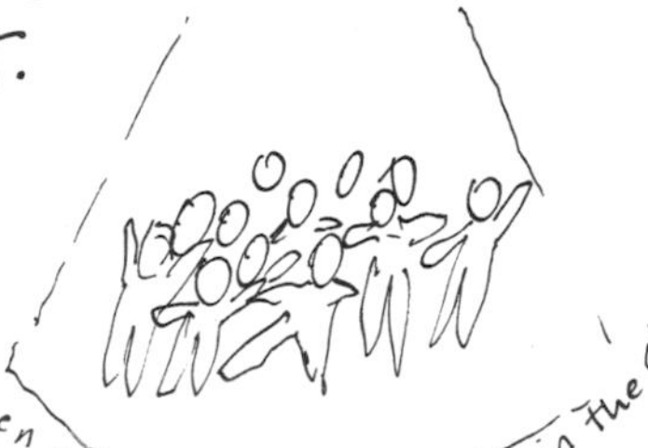
Then we can dance together in the glowing

I keep building barricades, hiding from pain, distracting myself from agony, and then I wrench myself out of my illusion of safety and face the work.

- What wakes you at 3 A.M. and feels scary?
- What is your darkest fear?
- How do you hide from dark places?
- What does investigating the darkness sound like to you?

"When you face pain directly she will give you an ointment so the wounds don't fester."

Ruth Gendler

If we use a flashlight while investigating the darkness, we will have a guiding beacon. Perhaps we can shine it on neglected parts that need light or be aware that many others are in the darkness, stumbling and exploring.

My therapist also talks a lot about holding the parts of myself that are wounded or crippled. I usually turn away and resist. Sometimes I do try, and I cradle something ugly in myself and watch it soften and transform.

I have seen terrifying sadness transform with the cradling.

Women's Hearts Are Big enough to Bear the pain, peer into the Dark, and do the work.

We Are led into Darkness anyway by events of Life: Death, loss, and pain. We cannot pretend that we don't live with the Darkness, or smile it away or think somehow we will escape.

There is no need to escape!

"The Light at the end of the tunnel is a Freight Train. Only God is Driving."

SARK

I will Be in the Darkness too! We Are not Alone and our Healing touches everyone.

our Hearts Are really very close together.

We Are All Aching, seeking, Breathing, crying and Hoping...

I send you the welcoming of the Dark

Blocks to Succulence

Being present in the Darkness by Cheri Huber
The Highly Sensitive Person by Elaine Aron PH.D
embracing your inner critic by Hal Stone PH.D & Sidra Winkelman Stone PH.D
Understanding the Enneagram by Don Richard Riso
Wishcraft by Barbara Sher with Annie Gottlieb
Procrastination by Jane Burka PH.D & Lenora Yuen PH.D
Stand Still Like the Hummingbird by Henry Miller
For Henry Miller newsletter call 408 667 2574
Living Juicy by SARK
You Can Heal Your Life by Louise Hay
Change your Handwriting, Change your Life by Vimala Rodgers
Wouldn't Take nothing for my Journey now by Maya Angelou
Life Doesn't Frighten Me Poem by Maya Angelou Paintings by Jean-Michel Basquiat

resources

- intuitive solutions, "A set of 3 new cards that help you think through difficulties, make decisions in harmony with your values and integrity, and take inspired and effective action." By co-creators Joy Drake & Kathy Tyler of innerlink Associates 206·937·0738

Music

- Magical Child by Michael Jones
- Watermark by Enya

Feeling Safe as a Woman

I remember reading a book called Places in the World a Woman Could Walk. It was fiction, but the title really spoke to me about feeling safe. I feel unsafe a lot of the time, and when I walk alone (especially after dark), I know that luck and denial play a part in my carefully constructed "illusion of safety."

I was walking at the beach the other day with two friends, to watch the sunset. A woman approached us and told us that she felt nervous, that she thought someone was following her. She said,

"It was a black Chevy Blazer, and he went by me really slow about 5 times. So I went into the woods over there to hide, and men were saying really scary things to me there! So I ran out. Could I just walk with you?"

We drove her home, and I told her never to hesitate to ask for help—that if you have a "funny feeling," it usually means that something is going on.

Being stalked or followed by someone and feeling like prey is a horrible feeling. Sometimes, men don't understand it. Smaller or shorter men get a taste of it. It's a primitive thing, to feel like a target.

I pray for the safety of women all over this world

I'm glad that so many self-defense classes are being taught now. especially the ones that use full impact against padded, trained instructors who actually assault you. The theory is to retrain our bodies to fight in perilous situations, by reprogramming what we've been taught, have lived with, or think.

I'm working up my courage to take one of these classes. I think they need to be taught in junior high and high school.

Another way to feel safe is to talk about feeling unsafe. If we use our voices to describe, explain, ask other people for help— this subject will be a part of our conversations and not secret or hidden like the crimes themselves are.

Ultimate safety lies in the acceptance of safety as an illusion. We can prepare, train, fight, defend, study, or carry a large weapon and none of it guarantees our safety.

I am cautious, fairly informed, use my intuition, avoid certain areas, always lock my car doors— and I still walk alone at night. We all bargain with what we can and can't accept living with.

Women victims...
Are NOT

Beginning Ways You Can Fight Back

- Practice yelling "NO!" loudly from the bottom of your stomach. Many women are weak "No" sayers.
- Contact a self-defense class and ask if you can attend a graduation ceremony for a demonstration.
- Read about violence against women.
- Talk to other women and men about safety. The more that we collaborate with silence, the more that violence can grow.
- Be aware that in public places "being nice" has no place. If you get into an elevator and feel weird with another person, <u>get out</u>— with no thought of politeness. Almost every victim of attack has had a funny feeling right before violence occurred.
- Walk boldly and confidently. Project an aura of "Dont mess with me."
- Study how victims are developed and how you might be participating in a victim mentality.
- Pray and meditate for change.

<u>I</u> wish for all of us the lessening of violence against women and, eventually, the disappearance of this particular form of violence as we become trained, empowered, and society wakes up.

Going out Alone

I call them "captive women." They never go out without a man, or a group of women. If questioned about going out alone, they make squeamish faces and say,

"I couldn't go out *alone*. It wouldn't be any fun."

Even women who are not like this are shy about going out alone. There is still a social stigma about being out "alone" (translation: boring, desperate, nobody likes her). Going out alone is a skill and an art that can be learned, shared, and implemented.

When I go to restaurants alone and the host greets me with, "Just *one*?" I smile and say, "Oh—one is more than enough—you'd be surprised." Then I sometimes explain that simply saying "Table for one?" is more gracious and welcoming.

What you can bring along to assist you in being alone confidently:

Tools:

Dear
I Shock Myself by Beatrice Wood

Something to write in/on
Something to read

Attitude: confidence, curiosity, openness.

Don't worry if you don't feel any of these—just act "as if."

I go out alone to bars, restaurants, movies, events, on walks, and have traveled alone extensively.

If you learn and practice an attitude of confidence and take your own tools, you will begin to feel more free in the world, to go anywhere by yourself and create your own magic.

if you already know how to do this, please help other women learn it!

Practice saying this: I am welcome everywhere. A place is lucky to have me visit it.

another useful skill is talking to strangers—striking up a conversation is an art to practice. Some of it involves mild eavesdropping, which we are taught not to do, and most of us do anyway. You simply find people that interest you, and find a spot to comment, ask a question, or deliver a compliment. Most people are receptive. If not, you'll feel it right away and can busily read or write something as a diversion.

I have also made fake phone calls from pay telephones to seem like I had a "purpose"

One time, I spoke to a man in a bar wearing a leg cast and a safari suit. He turned out to be the son of a famous author, who had been raised by living in hotel suites all over the world.

We drank very expensive old port and I listened to his travel stories for most of the afternoon—the stories and the man were fascinating.

port

The label looked like it had come from a pirate ship—torn & yellowed very Authentic

We cannot meet or be met if we don't speak up, or take a chance. How can you deny someone the pleasure of meeting you?

let's all boldly talk to new people!

We Are not Alone in this World.

It just seems that way sometimes.

My Friend, Robin, who recently turned 40, just told me that she's started going out alone for the first time in her life, and that she loves it. "The freedom to go alone happily to the movies is marvelous."

Take yourself out on a date. Get all dressed up and go somewhere expensive. People will stare and wonder, "Who is that fascinating woman?"

I used to send so many customers to this elegant restaurant in the Bahamas that they set up a table just for me. I would come in with my sketchbook and sit alone. I always met people and had conversations.

A sketch book is a fine dinner companion

You are fabulous and interesting all by yourself

Besides, if more and more women go out all by themselves, we'll begin to see each other, and can join each other's tables!

I promise you this: if you develop your abilities in going out alone, you will begin to forget that you're out by yourself! It will also double your chances of meeting a romantic interest— if you're by yourself.

Traveling is another dimension of going out alone. It takes a kind of intrepid faith.

Go! See the world! Take solitary walks and meet other kindred spirits.

Bring your walking stick and speak with the wood spirits

Being self-entertaining

I call them "self-entertaining units"— women who can visit you and function well by themselves. I used to have houseguests that hovered near me with plaintive eyes and whining requests. "What should I do now?"

We can develop self-entertaining skills. Women are taught to cling and cluster and need to redevelop the ability to be self-entertaining and independent.

Attitude:
- Keen interest in others and environment
- exploratory mode
- Ability to collect stories along the way
- open eyes
- Fresh mind (everything is new)

Equipment:
- Journal/sketchbook 
- letter writing kit 
- walking shoes 
- Books 

Expand your self-entertaining equipment by including whatever you like that you can do alone, or share with others.

There is bravery and confidence involved in being self-entertaining, yet the more you develop these skills, the more others will want to be with you!

We can all think of fascinating women who are always off exploring something— the world provides for these women by opening doors to brand new experiences.

THIS WAY TO A Brand new experience

One of the reasons we depend upon others for entertainment is because we don't trust ourselves to provide it.

When was the last time:

- You deliberately got lost in your car?
- Called a brand new person?
- Went on an exploring walk with no destination?
- Took yourself out for an exquisite dinner?
- Planned a solitary trip/retreat?
- Had a serendipitous adventure?
- Went by yourself to a movie?

Being self-entertaining is a gift you give to yourself and others.

The gift is you!
Can you find the scissors in this bow?

Now my houseguests bring me stories and presents from their adventures out in the world!

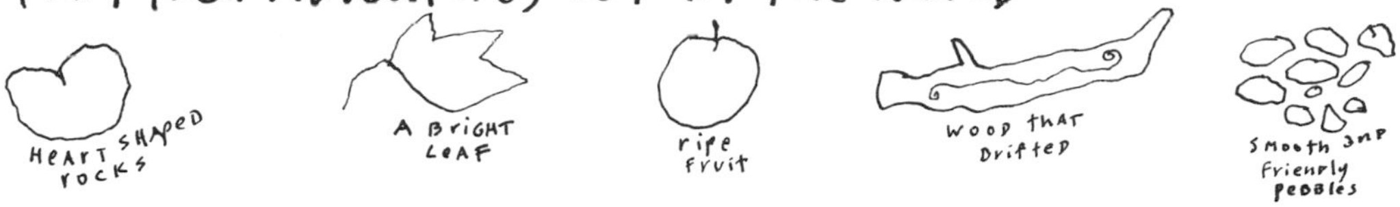
Heart shaped rocks
A bright leaf
ripe fruit
wood that drifted
smooth and friendly pebbles

Entertain yourself well—you will be surprised at what a good guest you are.

Remember: the real luxury is in your interior.

Fear of Being "too much"

All my life, I've heard that I'm "too much." Too wild, Too loud, too outrageous, too emotional, too sensitive, Too needy,

TOO MUCH

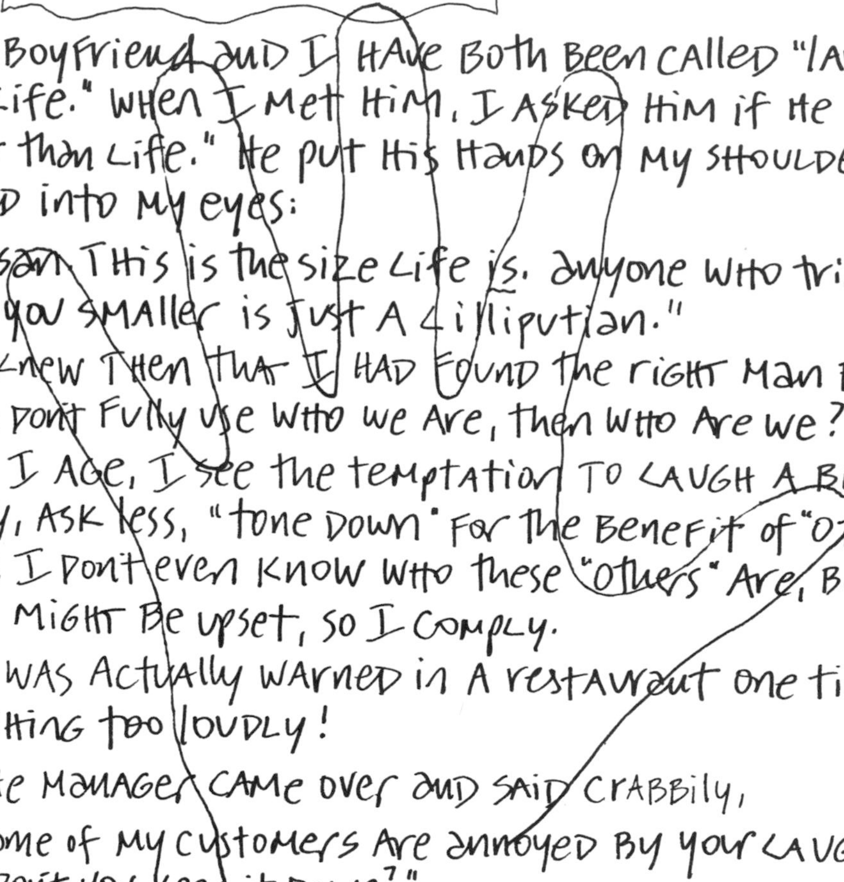

My Boyfriend and I have both been called "larger than life." When I met him, I asked him if he felt "larger than life." He put his hands on my shoulders and looked into my eyes:

"Susan, This is the size life is. anyone who tries to make you smaller is just a Lilliputian."

I knew then that I had found the right man for me. If we don't fully use who we are, then who are we?

As I age, I see the temptation to laugh a bit less loudly, ask less, "tone down" for the benefit of "others." often I don't even know who these "others" are, but They might be upset, so I comply.

I was actually warned in a restaurant one time for laughing too loudly!

The manager came over and said crabbily,

"Some of my customers are annoyed by your laughter— Why don't you keep it down?"

I asked who these customers were. He refused to say, so I stood up and said,

"Could I see a show of hands of people that are upset by the sound of my laughter?"

I was not laughing very loudly.

No one raised their hands, so I said to the manager, "Good. The matter is settled."

So, let's risk wearing something that's a bit "too much," laughing "too much," and loving "too much."

Write and tell me if you've ever been told you're too much, and we'll start a society:

THE TOO MUCH SOCIETY
We'll have too much parades!

Certainly, we'll wear hats that are too much, and eat too much chocolate

and then we'll take too many naps!

OLD, Alone, and Succulent

I met my friend's mother. She is in her 70's and very feisty. We had a tea party, she and I and her son, and when they were leaving, I told her she was a succulent wild woman.

"How?" she asked, her eyes flashing. Her son looked nervous. This fueled my answer.

"By the way you flung your head back while lying on my chaise lounge, by the way you tried on my painted silk cape with such flair and style."

She has lots of flair and style

Her son was blushing, and his mother said, "I'll have you know that I danced alone the other morning — the jitterbug! I haven't forgotten at all."

If we marry our fears — being old and being alone — we come up with the terrifying phrase, "old and alone." Yet, why is it so terrifying?

We're all getting older everyday. One day, we will be old women. We can be fabulous old women, or crabby, unwilling old women. It's our choice:

let's all be fabulous old women!

Sometimes age brings health challenges. We can meet these challenges with love or resistance, allowing or rejecting. Of course, it isn't always easy.

We are studying now to be the old women we will be. Take the right courses, give yourself tests. We can welcome any alone-ness and magnify the goodness in it. Celebrate the great parts of being alone.

Our Fears turn "OLD and Alone" into a nightmare. We must live in our dreams and know that old and alone is nothing to fear.

We will be succulent wild old women!

"The problem comes when we want to cling to a particular thought or idea. The mind always wants to cling. I'm 60 years old, and if I'm still clinging to being 40, then I'm in trouble."

RAM DASS

My mother is facing living alone at age 73 after the death of her husband and the end of their 46-year marriage. She dearly misses him, and their life together.

She has also begun to see some blessings.

The other day she called to tell me she was planning her new bathroom in her new home, and said,

"Pink towels! I'm going to finally have pink towels. I've always wanted them, but didn't think it was fair to your dad to have such a feminine bathroom."

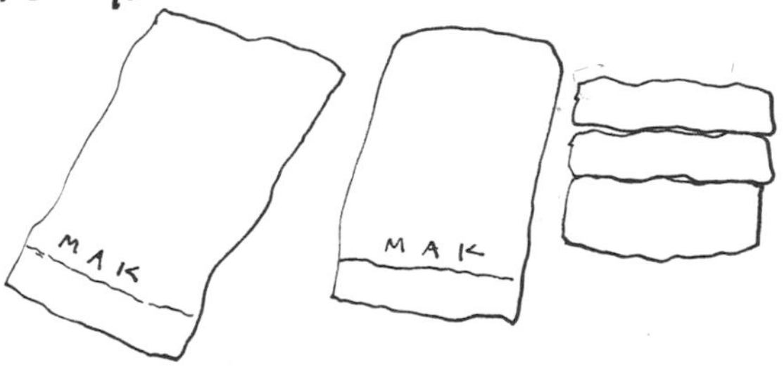
MAK
MAK

THICK
THIRSTY
perfectly
pink
Towels

We all have our versions of pink towels!

Fears

Dancing in The Flames By Marion Woodman
Love is letting Go of Fear By Gerald Jampolsky
The Fear Book By Cheri Huber
The Crone By Barbara G. Walker
Awakening the Warrior within By Dawn Callan
Women who run with the Wolves By Clarissa Pinkola Estes Ph.D
How you do anything is How you do everything By Cheri Huber
To order call 415 967-3710
Growing OLD is not For Sissies By Etta Clark
Two or Three Things I Know For sure By Dorothy Allison
Persephone returns By Tanya Wilkinson
Playing Chess with The Heart By Beatrice Wood Photos by Marlene Wallace
Warrior Marks By Alice Walker
Schoolgirls By Peggy Orenstein

resources

- rAinn, the rape, Abuse and incest national network, A multilingual, 24 hour counseling and support hotline, 800-656-HOPE
- national domestic violence hotline, A crisis intervention support for victims and their families and friends. Multilingual, 24 hours, 800-799-SAFE
- For a copy of Gary Rosenthal's poem "The Museum of the Lord of Shame" (11 page book) send $3, which includes postage to, Point Bonita Books, 5920 Dimm Way, Richmond, CA 94805

Music

- Migration by Peter R. Kater and Carlos Nakai

Importance of Being Crabby

Could we all just admit when we're crabby? My mother used to answer the phone in a fake cheerful voice, "Hellloooo!" right after yelling at us.

answering the phone was more important than how you felt

So often, we "put on a happy face," "grin and bear it," "Smile—it can't be that bad." sometimes it can be!

Being crabby is real and it's healing. It can help us get closer to what's wrong, or what hurts.

If you say to a friend, "I'm just crabby right now," they can usually tell anyhow, and sometimes it opens up a dialogue. If you say to other women, "Are you crabby?" they usually love it.

I like doing this on the phone with service providers who sound crabby. If you say something, it gives them permission to be human, and can result in a fabulous, honest exchange.

Crabbiness dissolves with the right kind of attention. Of course, there is also overcrabbiness, rampant crabbiness, or what my mother calls "the Crabby Appletons" (people who are crabby for a living and want to stay that way).

Remember to be crabby consciously! Women are great at being crabby and can do much more celebrating about it.

CRABBY and PROUD

FLY A CRABBY FLAG!

Self Healing

We all have the ability to self-heal. Whatever we've done, we can be forgiven. In our essences, we are truly innocent.

What does essence look like? A glowing, spinning orb?

I'm a survivor of sibling incest, physical abuse, rape, and am "almost an alcoholic." I've taken most "recreational" drugs and been on welfare. I've attempted suicide. I've binged on food and explored my codependency. I'm moderately neurotic and am currently examining my narcissistic structure. I have tendencies to be depressed, worry, and see things negatively.

I've been rebirthed, psychologically evaluated, in therapy, massaged, chakras cleared, psychically healed, had acupuncture for emotional reasons, read many, many self-help books, attended workshops, classes, talks about the inner child, the dysfunctional family, AA meetings, OA meetings, Alanon meetings, met with healers, listened to channelers, had out-of-body experiences, studied A Course in Miracles, been hypnotized and floated in sensory deprivation tanks.

There's more, but this list is making me tired!

Currently, I'm in individual therapy and group therapy. I still read self-help books, but not as compulsively. I practice meditation and mostly love my life.

I pray a lot.

Every time I meditate, there is resistance. Usually, I can welcome it. Sometimes not.

I have pretty healthy adult friends, and am in love with and loving a man who is becoming my partner and best friend.

I'm doing work that I love and living many of my dreams.

I am continuing to self-heal the wounds and holes left over from earlier life. I cry more, feel deeper, and have more tools to navigate through tough times with.

Some holes are larger than others... some are caverns...

"I'm no longer afraid of storms, for I am learning how to sail my own ship."

Louisa May Alcott

Explore healing options. If you feel unloved, look to yourself for love. Whatever the issues are, ultimately self-love and acceptance are the answers.

We all have tiny, mis-shapen parts of ourselves that we hide away and don't love. Turn towards those parts and cradle them.

I know and believe strongly that we are each our own best healers. Sometimes we need guidance or other people to activate our self-healing.

Give yourself the gifts of self-healing.

Your presence is the actual gift.

Therapy

Women are receptive to therapy, I think, because of their attention to the emotional aspects and need to be heard. I'm always amazed when women don't try, or haven't tried, therapy. Who else will listen so raptly to you?

Ideally we would all be assigned some kind of spiritual advisor at birth. We could turn to this person all through our lives for perspective, guidance, and free advice. Some of us already have this in a parent or grandparent. The rest of us could have an "internal grandmother."

There is still a stigma about "going to therapy," as though there is something wrong with you, or it is self-indulgent to pay someone to help you with psychological work. Yet we pay our car mechanics, our gynecologists, or gardeners. This is curious. What is more important than our psychological health?

I watch women repeating patterns, acting unconsciously, or lost in depression and wonder why they don't seek help. Often women will say, "I don't know any good therapists."

Helping hand

Sometimes we are stuck in a maze of our own making and could use a helping hand

Perhaps not, but other women do. Ask them. Therapy can be the acceleration out of a stagnant pattern, the support needed for an important change, the guidance for rebuilding self-esteem.

stagnant pattern

she rode away
from stagnation

Friends can also provide some of these things, but it's not their profession. A dedicated therapist's only professional purpose is your psychological health.

A large percentage of women have been sexually or physically abused—some of these women have never received any kind of therapy. I was one of these women. It took a failed suicide attempt and a brave friend asking, "Why aren't you in therapy?" (Thank you, Lisa!)

We can be those brave friends for each other.

A
Tribe
of
Brave
Friends

When I started therapy, it was terrifying to sit in a small room with a woman I didn't know, feeling exposed and

Telling Her My Secrets.

Now I've Been in therapy For 8 years, Both individual and Group work. I continue to go not because I have problems, but because it enriches me, and I am growing. I'm also fascinated by psychological process work.

We contain so much as women. We are so complex, stuffed full of feelings, memories, half-truths, denials, hopes, and yearnings.

We Deserve to Be Fully Alive psychologically!

Celebrate your own psychology!

explore your own interior
SHARE WHAT YOU FIND IN THERE
read words from your soul
YOU Are VALUABLE
JUST AS YOU ARE

 remember: Healing is an inside job

Healing Places

We heal from the inside, in certain outside locations. Here are some of my favorites:

Ocean: Waves remind us that there are reliable patterns like our breath. Also, the negative ions in the air actually change brain waves.

Woods: We are surrounded by tree families and sheltered by their canopies. Keep hugging trees.

Rocks: We are reminded that growth and change can be microscopic and result in something solid.

Waterfalls: Falling water speaks of constancy and power.

Gardens: In the gardens, our hands touch the growing things and our hearts fill.

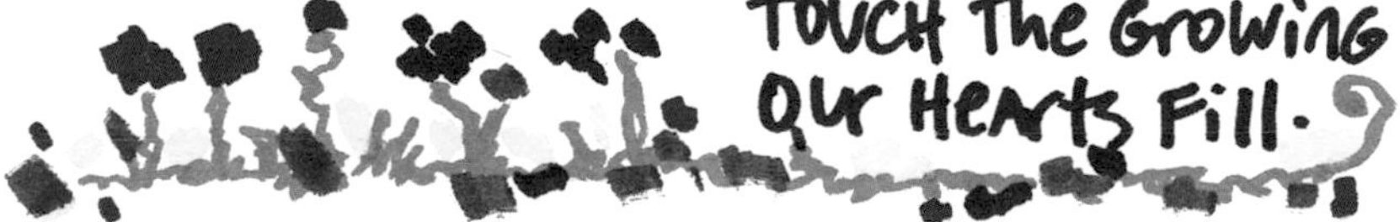

Tops of Hills: Overlooking the world, we see tiny cars or towns and gain perspective.

We also heal in inside locations. Here are some of my reliable spots:

BATHTUB: Floating in warm water, surrounded on all sides, tears can flow out of us and join the water everywhere.

Beds: soft and thick, safe places to hibernate and dream.

Forts: tiny nooks of privacy and escape. remember the safety of a good fort?

Phones: Psychic sound chambers, one on one, intimate conversations can take place without distraction.

Groups: in certain kinds of groups, there can be profound safety and exploration in the company of others.

planes: Speeding through the sky in a metal capsule emphasizes the importance of Trust and release of control.

Closets: in the back of the closet is a tiny door. Through there lies narnia . . .

In our hearts is where the healing occurs. We can take what we experience in the outside, and bring it in for healing.

Women's hearts are rare, deep and wide. We do contain multitudes!

I send you radical self-acceptance, power-full healing, and the miracle of your heart speaking— and you listening.

A room of your own

Women need space to be creative. Creativity thrives in solitude. It can be a tiny space.

When I was 10 years old, my grandfather had a little house built for me and delivered on a flatbed trailer. It had electricity, sliding glass windows, and a Dutch door.

I immediately "moved in" and began cooking creative projects. It was my sacred creative spot.

Now I'm 42 and live in the "Magic Cottage." It's a 180-square-foot former tool shed, and not much bigger than the playhouse of my childhood. I have bells on the door that I put out when visitors are welcome. When the bells aren't out, nobody can knock. This gives me privacy and solitude for creativity.

Women live such accessible and intimate lives—we are often physically or psychically open to other people. It is even more important, then, to have "rooms of our own."

Special thanks to Virginia Woolf, who wrote about a room of one's own.

My friend Kathryn was living in an apartment with her husband and very young son, and craved a space in which to create. She put up a tent in the corner of the apartment, and stuffed it full of her jewelry supplies, doll making materials, and other creative treasures.

A fort full of creativity

We all have odd, unused spaces that could be turned into creative retreat spots.

Creativity suffers under close scrutiny—ours or someone else's.

We all need a space of our very own that is like the soup pot—always simmering and getting better with age.

What's in your soup pot?

Give yourself space to lay out paper, leave paints in a scatter, a few beads on a scrap of velvet, a bit of wood that blew in from the sea.

i love you

Nourish your eye and spirit with inspiring things. They will bloom with your tending.

Things to try for Healing

There are so many tools and resources for healing available to us as women. Begin to keep your own "Healing Book" of things you have tried, or would like to try— then, share your list!

THE
HEALING
BOOK

Sometimes just reading the list feels healing to me

Here is a list from my Healing Book:

long solitary hike
comet watching
Moon bathing
telephone support
Breaking things
letters never sent
rituals, Burnings
Motherpeace Tarot
Giant Bubble Bath
poem writing
collage making
Meditation
crying
journaling

What feels healing to you?

More from the
Healing Book

Hot springs
i ching
rune stones
Acupuncture
sage, incense, candles
throwing things away
inner child cards
transformation game
angel cards
Bach flower remedies
drumming
sweat lodges, saunas, hot tubs
healing places
reading healing words
hiding
complaining to someone with no solutions offered
laughing until your stomach hurts
listening to audio tapes
healing videos
visiting an inspiring person
telepathically communicating with an animal
being of service
going to a movie in daytime, by yourself
prayer
more tears

We are not alone in our healing work!

How to Forgive Your Father

I AM not DADDY's little Girl.
I'M A Mountain lion in A Skirt, with prayers in my Heart.

When I Asked my DAD what He wanted in A "Dream Daughter," He Said,
"I wanted A Daughter who would wear an Apron and make soup from A HAM Bone."
I'M A vegetarian who Doesn't cook.
My "Fantasy Father" would Be super literary and work At Home.
My DAD WAS A traveling salesman who struggled with spelling.
When I was 4, my DAD's Head was as Big As The world! I rode on His shoulders, clasping His forehead with my tiny Hands and laughing as we ran through the grass.
Together we were taller than God.
My DAD Held my red Schwinn Bike As I Balanced My First solo trip, and ran Alongside Before letting Me Go to pedal into A new world.
My DAD Always Got MAD At Dinner and I Thought it was Because of me so I sat up straight and tried to Do it All perfect and He still yelled. His DAD Got MAD At Dinner too.
I Finally learned that when I could show softness, my DAD could show support. I wish I'd HAD More time to Be with Him. I remember whisker rubs and "serious talks" and standing on His Feet to Dance Around The Kitchen. He tied my ice skates Double-tight, and There was Always Love—Large and raw and imperfect. When I prowl through all the prayers in my Heart, and in certain photographs in A special kind of light, I can see my DAD's Face inside my own, saying, "Stick with me, Kid!"
I know now that He loves me in His language—that the past stuff is just Fog on the mirror—that the little Girl inside never stopped loving Him. She Feels the love and Forgives the pain.

Hey DAD! I'll love you Forever, you know.

©SARK 97

in memory of Arthur James Kennedy ♥

Healing

Beginning to Heal
By Ellen Bass & Laura Davis
Legacy of the Heart
By Wayne Muller
Healing into Life and Death
By Stephen Levine
The Inner Child Workbook
By Cathryn Taylor
On Death and Dying
By Elisabeth Kübler-Ross
The Miracle of Mindfulness
By Thich Nhat Hanh
No Enemies Within
By Dawna Markova Ph.D.
I Know Why the Caged Bird Sings
By Maya Angelou
A God Who Looks Like Me
By Patricia Reilly
Anatomy of the Spirit
By Caroline Myss Ph.D.
The Courage to Heal
By Ellen Bass & Laura Davis
I recommend the movie, Harold and Maude.

Resources

- Voice Dialogue and the Psychology of Selves tape series. By Hal Stone, Ph.D. and Sidra Winkelman Stone Ph.D. c/o Delos, PO Box 604 Albion, CA. 95410 Call for a catalog 707·937·2424
- Sounds True catalog recordings, learning tapes for the inner life. For information: Sounds True Catalog, PO Box 8010, Boulder CO. 80306 Call 303·665·3151
- Neon Play-Doh

Music

- The Good Omens Tape/Chanting the Vimala Alphabet, Institute of Integral Handwriting Studies, 205 13th St., Ste. 3191, SF, CA 94103. To order, call 888·813·9400. Price $7.50 + .50 for tax and shipping.
- The Memory of Trees by Enya
- Neroli by Brian Eno

Adventuring without Money

I wish for women to explore the world and open as many doors as possible. There are many ways to have adventures with little or no money, and lots of creative thinking.

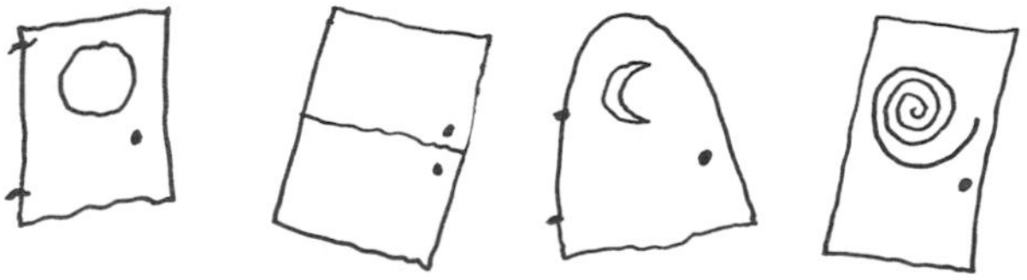

There are many doorways to adventure

During my twenties, comfort meant very little so I traveled with tiny amounts of money and lived day to day. Islands were most intriguing to me, so I found ways to visit and live on them.

I slept on chaise lounges by the pool, taught swimming lessons, baby-sat, house-sat, or accepted hotel rooms from managers who admired my spirit.

I spent a lot of time on Paradise Island, in the Bahamas. The turquoise water is translucent blue and the sand is shocking white, or the color of chocolate chip cookie dough. There are bright green casuarina pine trees and sudden giant clouds.

casuarina pines are soft and feathery

There are statues of strong women with moss in their armpits and lizards in their hair. Things are slightly unkempt and crumbling in the islands. Secrets abound.

Wild cats come out to eat the scraps of food from fancy restaurants. The men and women are golden and laugh easily.

One of the costs of adventuring is that you are faced with your<u>self</u>. You cannot escape by going to a job and doing lots of activities. Having little money promotes contemplation.

Sometimes what you find inside of yourself is not easy to look at.

Mostly I ate mangoes naked, went barefoot through the hibiscus petals, slept helplessly for countless hours, pinned to my bed by transformative dreams. I also felt desperately lonely in paradise, and like my life had become a humid tropical failure.

One of my favorite ways to adventure was to keep moving—so I went to explore Jamaica.

Jamaica is a wonderland for succulence, and for women. In the islands, people are ripe. Like the fruit.

I spent a number of beatific months living in Ocho Rios, Jamaica. I called everyone I knew and told them I was staying forever.

Jamaica was the closest thing I'd ever seen to the movie, Swiss Family Robinson and my dream of living in a treehouse.

I met a man named Bongo Silly who lived in a treehouse, and rented rooms in the branches—he had dozens of pairs of Keds tennis shoes, in all different colors,

and cooked unbearably delicious soup.

I sat at a table made from a door, my bare feet on clay earth, and ate soup out of a seashell with a hand-carved wooden spoon.

I also met a man who lived beneath a waterfall in a cave that had glittering walls. His name was Fuck-up, and his specialty was grilling vegetables that he grew himself. To get to his cave, you had to wade across a river and climb on smooth stones warmed by the sun.

The smooth stones warmed by the sun

Both of these men were not "educated" in the ordinary sense, and I learned that spirituality often lives in simplicity.

There were many mysteries in Jamaica, and I went eagerly from one to another, tasting all that I found.

I thrived in the barefoot, outdoor living that I found in the islands — wearing bright bits of cloth and being in the sea. I learned a lot about my physical self in these places.

There was a freedom in the way of life that opened me

Another outrageous adventure I always wanted to experience was living in New York City. When I was in my early twenties, and still living in Minneapolis, I became intrigued by the subject of obscene phone calls. I began collecting research for a book by interviewing the callers.

Nobody had ever done this. I placed ads in newspapers across the United States that read, "If you make obscene phone calls, call me."

The results were fascinating, and I asked my best friend at the time to join me in my trip to New York.

We rode our bicycles from Minnesota to New York with the accumulated research. When we arrived in New York City, I called the New York Post and told them to send a writer and photographer (the pictures turned out to be too revealing to print in the paper).

Then I called The Washington Post and told the story to columnist Maxine Cheshire. She did her whole column on the story of the "Book," front page.

This got us into Doubleday to meet with their senior editor. We sold the book idea by telling stories. He arranged for us to stay in various empty penthouse apartments while we tried to write "The Book."

working title: CALLS of the WILD

Instead, we partied with millionaires, appeared on radio and TV, and talked all the time about "The Book." It was exhausting, and we weren't writing anything. Then our friendship developed problems while trying to collaborate.

We finally turned in a proposal after Doubleday threatened to cut off access to our penthouses (this had gone on for a year!).

Doubleday responded:

"This is the worst book proposal we have ever seen in all of our years of publishing—but, we want to see anything else you write because there is a certain energy."

I didn't even hear the second part. It was my worst fear come true. I wasn't really a writer,

I'd failed, I'd never publish, and there was no hope for me.

I left New York soon after that, and moved back to Minneapolis, and moved into the little playhouse my grandfather had built for me.

Mice
From
Mars

I'd written my first book in this playhouse at age 10, and thought I'd try writing everyday and see if I was really a writer.

It was desperate and difficult and I don't know how I managed to continue—but I did. The worst thing was that my writing bored me!

During my thirties, my adventures were more in my own interior as I lived the life of a "starving artist" trying to find her creative place in the world.

I believe it is important to continue having outrageous adventures all through our lives—in whatever forms they take.

Women can explore the world even more by bravely traveling alone, being willing to work along the way, arrange for fair trades and barters, rely on other women and friends, write about their experiences, share their stories, and en·courage other women to have more outrageous adventures!

My most outrageous adventure right now, at age 42, is learning to love and live intimately with another human being. I'll keep you posted.

Traveling Alone

All God's Children need Traveling Shoes

Maya Angelou

I envision a world filled with women traveling alone, and meeting each other on the path...

I love traveling alone for these reasons:

- The sense of adventure is very clear
- All my tastes and preferences are honored
- Meeting "strangers"
- sipping tea for hours
- no destinations but my own
- the sense that anything could happen

The challenging parts to traveling alone are:

- Being scared
- Feeling all alone
- relying only on yourself
- not meeting anyone

pack a bag with tiny treasures and favorite clothes that cheer you

Then I realized that I feel all these things when I'm home! Where have you always wanted to go? Plan a mystery trip to places you've always wondered about (the mystery part is mostly you.)

One time, I was traveling with a man I had met in Monte Carlo, and we were headed to Paris. Suddenly, I knew that I had to experience Paris by myself. I asked if he would mind splitting up and meeting again later. He felt offended by this request and stalked off the train.

As the train pulled out of the station for Paris, I felt nearly unbearable excitement at the idea of _me_ and _Paris_ meeting.

Shakespeare and Company

I went on to live in a bookstore—above the shelves, behind a purple velvet curtain, and across from Notre Dame Cathedral. I worked in the bookstore in exchange for rent.

I know that if I'd still been with my friend, this adventure would not have happened.

I had to
step into
my own story...

I have often felt called to journey by myself—and I'm not particularly brave either. In fact, I get homesick very easily, and sometimes just hide in my tent all day, eating cheese and chocolate for "company."

Dark chocolate
Swiss cheese

Yet, so many adventures speak to us when we travel alone. It's as though the adventure takes the place of a person.

Stretch your traveling alone muscle. Start with tiny trips, or leap into the glorious unknown of a big trip.

Where have you always wanted to go?

Don't wait! Travel alone...

Adventures Close to Home

Women deserve adventurous lives. As little girls, we served flower petals on plates made of leaves, and imaginary liquid in thimbles, wearing skirts made of old tablecloths.

The table might be an old tire

We adventured on our bicycles, which turned into imaginary horses. There were daily adventures, close to home, beneath the clothesline, in homemade forts, and in our best friends' bedrooms.

As adult women, we can become more sedate, less experimental—we develop "Adventure Amnesia" and don't even remember what is lost.

Then we're invited to a tea party and feel a fizz of excitement.

Come to
a tea party
with
remarkable
women.
Wear a hat.

Or, we take a "Miracle Walk" in our neighborhood—just to look at trees.

We go out dancing together and wear wild nail polish... (M and D, this is you!)

We remember our adventurous souls. I like to take my sleeping bag and drive to the country during comet active times. I hike to a hilly spot and watch shooting stars.

Full moon hiking is another grand adventure. Extending our antennae can produce adventures in "ordinary places."

While walking on a cliffside trail with my friend, Debbie, around the bend appeared a man in an elegant suit and tie— as though he had just walked out of a magazine. I complimented his appearance loudly and heartily, and he grinned and introduced us to his 2 Japanese friends, also wearing suits. They disappeared down the path, and we laughed at the incongruity of it.

A tiny adventurous moment, close to home. It changes your perspective, reminds you that the world is deep and rich and full of colors and miracles.

Fill your life with tiny and large adventurous moments.

Perfect peaches, lilting street musicians, a butterfly landing on your shoulder, happy dogs on the beach, people praying together outside, children wearing pajamas in the daytime, old women on benches, laughing.

These are all signs of adventure. 
Signs of Adventure

We must be open to adventure—seek it out, ask questions, dare to talk to strangers.

Women are oppressed by fears in this society. It's true. It's not safe. Neither is staying home, hiding from an adventurous life.

Take self-defense, use your intuition and caution, walk in pairs and groups, but please, come out of your houses, apartments, and cars.

Your Adventures Await You!

Outrageous Adventures

Tracks by Robyn Davidson
Don't Push the River by Barry Stevens
The Wonderful Flight to the Mushroom Planet by Eleanor Cameron
I Should Have Stayed Home edited by Roger Rapoport and Marguerita Castanera
Gutsy Women: Travel Tips and Wisdom for the Road by Marybeth Bond
The Air Conditioned Nightmare by Henry Miller
SARK's Journal and Play! Book by SARK
Maiden Voyages: writings of women travelers edited by Mary Morris in collaboration with Larry O'Connor
A Foxy Old Woman's Guide to Traveling Alone by Jay C. Ben-Lesser
Without a Guide: contemporary women's travel adventures edited by Katherine Govier
Travelers' Tales: A Woman's World by Marybeth Bond
The Size of the World by Jeff Greenwald
The Independent Woman's Guide to Europe by Linda White

resources

- The Transformation Game, Blessing Cards, intuitive solutions and Angel Cards. All wonder-full resources to inspire you! To order: Innerlinks Associates, Joy Drake and Kathy Tyler, co-creators, 704-665-9937, Address: P.O. Box 10502 Asheville, NC 28806 website: www.innerlinks.com
- Moonlight Chronicles: A wonder-full handwritten exploration of waking and looking at life. "Why are we here?" "Where is here?" PO Box 109, Joseph, Oregon 97846
- Bright rubber balls
- Ping Pong, a bi-annual publication by the Henry Miller Library, featuring writing and observations on Henry Miller, as well as literary pieces by local writers. Hwy 1, Big Sur, CA 93920 408-667-2574 / www.henrymiller.org
- Henry Miller Library, Highway 1, Big Sur, CA 93920 408-667-2574 "Serendipity in a redwood grove by the sea."

Music

- New Beginnings by Tracy Chapman

Movie

- Auntie Mame

Succulent Shy Women

I've had many varied sexual experiences, and I'm still shy sexually.

I want to honor myself and any other woman for being shy about expressing herself sexually, or describing what she needs or wants.

Succulence does not always mean wild abandon or juicy freedom—sometimes it is a quiet unfolding, a peeling back to reveal a tender center.

I know I've felt pressure to be sexually wild, free—like a warrior Aphrodite! Sometimes I've acted out others' fantasies and not my own.

Right now I'm exploring a softer, more vulnerable sexual me.

There is a shy part of me that wants long, quiet explorations with my sexual partner. Where you press your faces close together and share deep secret wishes before being sexual and where you can say,

"Slower please. Slower still."

Sometimes sexuality can seem so explicit or graphic—it can be scary. I'm allowing shyness to be present, to include it in my succulence.

Succulent shy woman

l e t ' s   w e l c o m e   o u r   q u i e t   p a r t s.

SUCCULENT SHY WOMAN WAKING UP

If you would like to explore your sexuality in less shy ways, here are a few suggestions:

Read erotic literature written by women. There are wonderfull poems and stories that can privately and quietly inspire you.

Watch videos or television programs that explore sexuality. Two tv programs I watch are: Real Sex (HBO) and Late Date (cable). Both shows are funny, intelligent, and immensely informative.

Draw a sexual map of your body in your journal: Describe your body sexually in great detail, as though you were creating an "owner's manual" for someone else to read. Consider sharing with a lover.

Let your sexual self write a letter: your sexuality has things to share with you that you may not be able to hear in ordinary circumstances. Start your letter: "What I need or want sexually."

Invite a lover to take a body tour of you. Light candles, blindfold him/her, and set a 15-minute timer. Explore only for this time. Switch if you feel like it.

Keep a sexual journal with your lover (or invent a lover). Write passages about what you want, or what you liked.

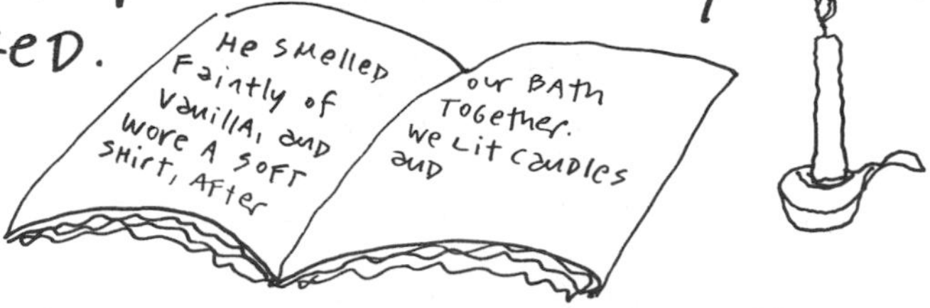
He smelled faintly of vanilla, and wore a soft shirt, after
our bath together. We lit candles and

Gently explore yourself sexually. Open new territories.

erotic robots

I've been an erotic robot. My definition is: using the body sexually without soul. Being an erotic robot also occurred when I would try to satisfy lovers in bed by doing things that satisfied only their fantasies— not my own. I felt like a performer, and would "leave my body" in order to function sexually.

When I look back at my times of being an erotic robot, I see a young woman plunging unknowingly into worlds of others' imaginations.

I was afraid to really know myself sexually, or be truly intimate with a partner. I am still afraid.

So many of my episodes sexually took place because I couldn't say no and wanted to be adored.

I sometimes made love just to "be polite" or to get it over with so the other person would go home! (Maybe if he comes, he'll go).

Once, I was seduced by advertisements for "erotic dancing." "perfect for artists and students, no touching permitted, let out your wild self!"

Perfect
JOB For
terrified,
lost SOULS
who Also
need Money

I was 22 years old, and for $20 an hour, it seemed perfect.

I couldn't figure out how to put on my G-string before dancing. Once on stage, I moved woodenly and like I was underwater. I remember a lot of men in plaid shirts yelling things at me. There was a lot of sadness and shame in the room.

It was awful and I quit that night.

There were other times I attempted to have a "sexpositive" experience by dancing or modeling erotically. They all failed.

I like the idea of taking the shame out of it, of women dancing erotically in a positive way. Until our culture fully embraces women, I'm not sure that it's possible to make that realm positive. Perhaps the women who are trying to change this will succeed—I hope so.

My experiences were shaming and soul-less. It taught me that my body is precious and not separate from my soul.

I thought I could make a lot of money fast, be outrageous and show off my dancing and body.

The fantasies and words of these men were not honoring or even fun. It felt desperate and very, very, very sad.

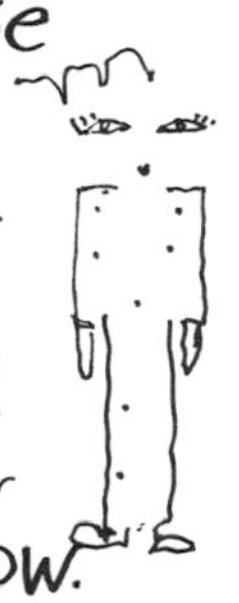

The erotic robot was a frozen performer

I've retired the erotic robot part of myself now. She stands mechanically in my memory as a reminder of how, as women, we are soft and irreplaceable and very human and alive—especially sexually.

I honor my times as an erotic robot and do not regret them (although I wouldn't mind erasing certain things).

Now there are much more fascinating things to learn and explore about myself sexually.

As women, we deserve to be erotically alive, exploring our sexual mysteries and yearnings.

My
Sexual
Mysteries

Vibrators

"Home is where I plug in my vibrator."

SARK

I got my first vibrator at age 21. It scared me, so I kept it in a shoe box in my dresser for quite awhile.

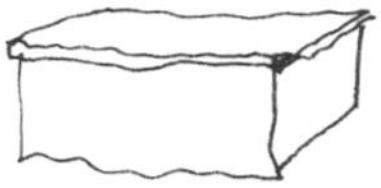

On Easter Sunday, I was supposed to visit my parents, and didn't really feel like facing the day, so I took out my vibrator.

I used a towel to cushion my skin from the machine (secretly I was afraid of being electrocuted), and proceeded to experiment.

Very quickly, and with fantastic shock waves, I experienced the most powerful, glorious orgasm I had ever had!

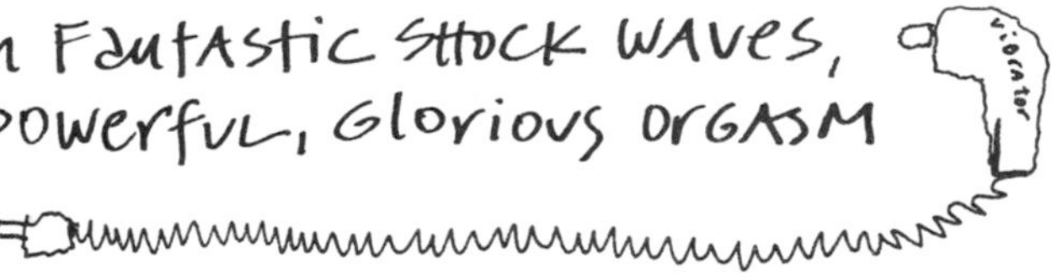

Why hadn't someone told me about this?

I felt quite startled and puzzled by the intensity, and after briefly recovering spent a lot of that afternoon practicing. Later, I bounded down the stairs of my house shouting,

"Happy, Happy Easter!!"

I continued practicing so much in the week after Easter that I became pale and rather exhausted. I finally shared my vibrator experiences with a girlfriend and confessed to having 50-60 orgasms in a day!

I've always been an extremist.

She pointed out that I might be overdoing it— just a bit. Ha!

And so, I am a committed vibrator user. I wish I'd had one when I was younger. I think it would have meant less awkward sex in the bushes with my first boyfriend.  and more orgasms for me!

The bushes were an "instant bedroom"

Note: vibrators are no better than, or capable of replacing, lovers. Have no fear!

Boys are "taught" and even encouraged to masturbate. Girls are not.

I was given a pink booklet about menstruation and warned about pregnancy. Nobody talked about pleasure— especially self-pleasure!

Your menstrual cycle

Why are we not taught and encouraged to pleasure ourselves as women?

I know women who have never had an orgasm. Then there are countries/cultures that perform genital mutilation and remove the clitoris so there can be no pleasure. read Warrior Marks by Alice Walker

The more we learn about our own bodies and orgasms, the more empowered we'll be to share sexual pleasures with a partner, and with ourselves.

Women deserve sexual pleasure!

Vibrators Are Good

Brave Wonderings

I wish for women: the freedom to sexually explore without shame. The ability to be conscious sexually. The awareness of self-pleasure, and knowledge of their sexual bodies and discovery of their "sexual spirituality."

I wonder if I have been so damaged by incest that I cannot be healthy sexually. I wonder if the years of unconscious self-destructive sex really taught me anything?

I wonder if I will ever feel truly at home in my body and at peace as a sexual creature.

I wonder if I will write openly about being bi-sexual, and if people will be intrigued, repulsed or horrified. I wonder if I will be horrified, repulsed or intrigued. Why don't I feel free to just be bi-sexual?

I wonder why we don't talk more about masturbation, the dark side of sex, and why women are often such sexual victims.

I wonder about shame and sex and how they're connected.

I wish for women:
The release of sexual victimization and the courage to stop violence and objectification of women. The creation of a sexually postive world where we can have open dialogues about our sexual wishes, hopes, fears, and dreams. The wisdom to speak openly with our children about sexuality—the facts and the mysteries, and everything in between. The gift of safety in sexuality. Sexual peace of mind.

Sexual Mis·steps

I first titled this "sexual mistakes" but then I realized that I don't believe in mistakes as much as mis·steps, stumblings.

Creative exploration will always result in mistakes, and if we fear those, we risk paralysis and a numb, "good girl" mentality.

Our morality may guide us in our sexual exploration. Is your morality yours, or the regurgitation of parents' and/or religious beliefs?

What are your sexual beliefs?

Do you believe:

- Women can be sexual only in marriage and/or relationship?
- Women can explore sexually by instinct?
- Heterosexuality is better than homosexuality or bisexuality? Different? How? Why?
- Sexuality should/not be openly discussed?
- Sexual health and happiness is a right or a privilege?
- Sexuality is natural and healthy?
- Sexual expression needs to be encouraged/repressed?

Write down your sexual beliefs. Question yourself. You have the right to explore yourself sexually.

I would like to see young women write sexual "mission statements" that could guide them in their discoveries sooner.

My initial beliefs about my sexuality were shaped by rebellion, pain, instant gratification, and naiveté.

What would your sexual mission statement include?

If we spend more time shaping our beliefs, and honoring those beliefs, our steps could become more sure on our sexual paths.

I think that all my mis-steps led me to uncover my sexual beliefs rather late in life (and I'm still uncovering!). As I stumbled, I grew.

I had no role models of vibrant, passionate, outspoken sexual women.

In high school I became known as a "slut" because I spoke openly about sex. I played strip poker, so I was a "bad girl" (usually I won and made the boys take their clothes off!). 
9
10
Joker

I wish I'd gotten therapy sooner to help me in exploring myself sexually.

I wish I could have told the truth sooner to all the lovers I was performing for. I wish I could have forgiven myself along the way for my mis-steps.

I wish that I'd learned a little earlier about shame and how to manage it.

In honor of the mis-steps, let's, as women, take responsibility for ourselves sexually, and emerge as positive, sexually alive role models. Perhaps I can be a role model too.

I send you the courage to make your own mis-steps and keep walking bravely forward.

"And remember, we all stumble, every one of us. That's why it's a comfort to go hand in hand."

Emily Kimbrough

Sexually Blossoming

My sexual past will no longer determine my sexual present.

I will learn to speak gently and specifically about my sexual needs and desires.

I will tell the truth faster sexually.

I will continue growing sexually and not stagnate out of fear or lack of knowledge.

I will take my sexual temperature often, and report findings to myself and to my partner.

I will learn more ways to be sexually intimate.

I wish for you an opening, a loosening of old judgments or fears, a sexual lightness and well being, sexual curiosity, and abundance.

May we open to the sun and let light into any dark places. May we allow the dark and learn from it. May we laugh during sex play and be sexually awake.

"You can clutch the past so tightly to your chest that it leaves your arms too full to embrace the present."

Jan Glidewell

What is it about sex? I'm afraid to admit my mistakes, my failings, the soft vulnerable spots that I'm polka-dotted with. I fear being too graphic. I fear scaring people. I fear scaring myself. I know so little sexually. How dare I write about it? Do I deserve to be sexually safe and happy? Why not? How can I inspire sexual bravery in myself and others?

Let's open our sexual closets and gently investigate and share the contents.

SEXUALITY

Allies in Healing
By Laura Davis
Awakening your sexuality
By Stephanie Covington Ph.D.
The Sexual Healing Journey
By Wendy Maltz
Women, Sex and Desire
By Elizabeth Davis
The Couple's Comfort Book
By Jennifer Louden
Soulful Sex
By Dr. Victoria Lee
150 Most Asked Questions About Midlife Sex, Love and Intimacy
By Ruth S. Jacobowitz
The Good Vibrations Guide to Sex
By Cathy Winks and Anne Semans
Sex for One
By Betty Dodson Ph.D.
For Each Other
By Lonnie Barbach Ph.D.
Femalia
Edited by Joani Blank

resources

- The Good Vibrations Store: Fun place to order a vibrator
  1210 Valencia, SF CA 94110, 415·974·8980 · Mail order catalog: 800·289·8423
- Louanne Cole Weston, Ph.D. Certified sex therapist and licensed marriage, family and child counselor. "Sex Matters" audio tapes and columns. 3025 Fillmore Street, Suite A, SF, CA 94123
  415·923·9180. E-mail: lcole@ix.netcom.com.
- Sex and Love Addicts, Anonymous
  PO Box 1964, Boston MA 02105, 617·625·7961

Music

- French Kiss, original motion picture soundtrack
- I'll Be Your Baby Tonight by Bernadette Peters
- Unplugged by Eric Clapton

Marrying Yourself

My boyfriend used to ask his mother, "How can I find the right woman for me?" and she would answer,

"Don't worry about finding the right woman—concentrate on becoming the right man."

We must become the women that we are first, before entering fully into a relationship (some women can do this work while in a good relationship).

So often, I just molded myself into whatever the relationship seemed to need or require.

One time, after a long-term relationship had ended, a friend challenged me and said,

"Can you just spend some time alone now?" I never really had!

The idea of being alone terrified me. So I got a cat. This helped.

Buddha said: "If you want to learn about love, start with plants and animals—they're easier."

I entered a long period of celibacy, therapy, and learning to fall in love with myself.

Learning to fall in love with yourself is an immense challenge—I'm still learning!

I began to have conversations with other women about being alone, and what it meant to us.

I met two wonder·full women at a party

We spoke of "celibate dating," of men friends, and mysteries of romance, of claiming our own time, of sculpting, jewelry design, and of the wonder of being happily alone, and how couples are sometimes held up as the ideal. I said,

"People don't talk about how much work it is to be a couple!"

One of the women said,

"When you're alone, you can create your own mythology and nobody challenges you. In a relationship, your own bullshit gets reflected back much quicker."

I found that society is mystified by women alone. We don't commonly celebrate alone·ness the way we celebrate couples. Nobody says,

"How's your love life? With yourself?"

For awhile, I noticed couples everywhere. Everyone seemed to be "in love" except me. Then I began to realize the gifts that learning to love myself gave.

Finally I wasn't waiting to be loved!

I took vacations alone, bought clothes for my tastes only, read books undisturbed, and turned off the phone for days at a time.

The silent phone

Then, it seemed time to be in union with myself, so I performed a metaphorical marriage, and promised to love and honor myself until the end.

What this meant was that instead of waiting to be married or partnered, I decided to marry myself in a ceremony by the ocean with a private ritual to celebrate.

Try this: Marry yourself. Create a small wedding in nature, or somewhere special to you. Invent your own vows or promises, buy yourself a ring and flowers. Love and honor yourself until the end of time!

I had truly stopped looking for a partner, and wrote in my journal how at peace I was, but if I was looking, this is the type of lover I would want:

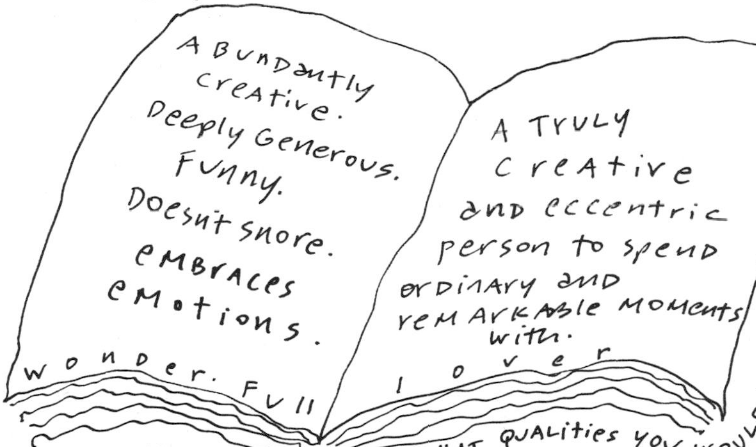

Abundantly creative.
Deeply Generous.
Funny.
Doesn't snore.
embraces emotions.
wonder. Full
A truly creative and eccentric person to spend ordinary and remarkable moments with.
lover

Try this: Make a list of what qualities you would want your soulmate to have

Then I also felt it was time to stop therapy, and began the process of termination. I said, "The only thing that could keep me in therapy would be if I fell in love."

The following week I met Craig. p.s. He snores.

Faces of Intimacy

Nobody tells us as little girls that we may fall in love and have moments of hating our beloved, or have ridiculous arguments at 2 A.M. over something neither person understands.

My friend John calls it, "the nuance of annoyance." After you've been with someone for awhile, all the tiny and large things they do that annoy you, come forward.

We are not taught something I call "intimate negotiations." It involves adjustment, compromise, integrity, truthtelling, options, willingness, and heart-full listening.

I watch friends who I admire in this area, and there is a softness, an inclusiveness in the way they speak.

union

Their goal is union.

I either isolate myself, or try to "take over" with loud suggestions, detailed directions, and rigid ideas. My goal is frequently BEING RIGHT.

My boyfriend sometimes calls me "Substitute Teacher Nancy," which is our signal that I've gone too far, or am marching to some non-negotiable drummer. (of course, he sometimes appears as a substitute teacher too!)

We often start over.

As I learn and navigate these intimate ways, there is a panic, or a kind of terror that sometimes arises: Am I doing it right? Being fair? Meeting my needs? Meeting someone else's needs? Expressing myself, yet maintaining appropriate emotional boundaries?

"Intimacy happens in moments. The mistake we make is in wanting it all the time."

JO ANN MAGDOFF

Actor Sharon Stone said, "Give me a thousand men in the audience, and me on the stage and I know exactly what to do. Give me just one man and me on a couch together, and I'm really scared."

Emotional storms pass through me frequently and since I generally try to resist most feelings as soon as I feel them, they tend to get stuck, be projected, or hoarded for attack later.

I envy the people I know who seem to communicate less out of their heads and more from their hearts (I'm working on allowing this!).

The "faces of intimacy" are all around us. They are infinitely more human than I ever thought.

Women deserve rich, emotional, intimate lives. We also need to understand ourselves intimately before we can recognize all the "faces of intimacy" and the many forms it takes.

I know that I'm in a process of letting go of romantic expectations and embracing new, tender, intimate moments that appear in ways I never imagined.

THE "GOOD GIRLFRIEND" MUST DIE

As I advanced in my love relationship, I began to notice an insidious part of my personality that seemed to arise often. I named her, "the good girlfriend," and this is what I wrote about her:

The "good girlfriend" always knows what to bring to a potluck, makes good potato salad, does all the communication tasks, makes her hair big and sexy, compromises about where to sit in the movies, is available, isn't "too serious," is sexy, doesn't say fuck, is available, blends with her partner, is assertive but fake, wears a pretty mask, is a "nice girl," shares feelings—but not too many!, seems spontaneous, but isn't, is angry, but says she's "annoyed," is full of rage, but says she's "upset," controls her feelings in a suitable container, doesn't change plans at the last minute, listens attentively, but is actually not present, looks sexy, yet doesn't live in her body, seems power. full but is actually power. less, doesn't dwell on unpleasant topics, buys the gifts, carefully controls atmosphere and environment, makes sure things are "pleasant," gives up when conflict feels thick, reveals only her best and finest qualities, does not fart audibly, definitely does not fart exuberantly, holds most feelings in and smiles through a tight and suffocating mask, always has effortless and pleasing orgasms.

the end!

I had absorbed years of conditioning about how I thought women needed to be so that someone would love them.

One day, my boyfriend and I had been invited to a barbeque, and the "good girlfriend" part of me became terrified at the thought of making potato salad and wearing something "cute," so I hid out and pretended to be sick. Craig found me in the bathtub and asked,

"Are you really sick? Or did you just not want to go to the barbeque?"

I burst into tears and said, "I can't be your girlfriend! I don't even know how to make potato salad..." I babbled on about all my faults and how I didn't feel "qualified" to be loved.

Craig held my hand, leaned over and said,

"You don't understand. I'm Captain Odd! We are perfect for each other. I don't even like potato salad! I don't care if you ever make it. I like you just as you already are."

I had connected love and performance together. Love is a mystery and doesn't keep score. We are worthy of love as women just as we are.

"Our limitations, our imperfections, our mistakes... these do not reflect our inferiority, but are part of being human."

Joan Sheingold Ditzion

Lessons in Love

"The first duty of love is to listen."

PAUL TILLICH

I feel like I've made lots of mistakes and learned lots of lessons in love. From my first boyfriend at 16 until now at 42, I figure I have 26 years of inexperience.

1970
1971
1972
1973
1974
1975
1976
1977
1978
and then we jump to . . .
1996
1997
and beyond . . .

I used to seek out married men so that they wouldn't expect too much from me. It wasn't until much later that I realized that I didn't think I deserved a "real relationship."

Commitment problems were something I continually blamed on men— much later I discovered that I was terrified of commitment, and covered this up by continually choosing "bad" men who weren't available.

sorry,
not
available

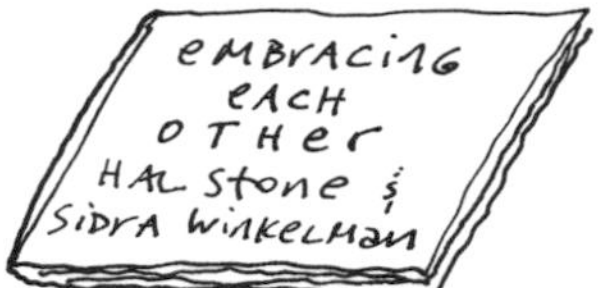
Embracing
Each
Other
Hal Stone &
Sidra Winkelman

There are so many excellent books now and people working to unravel problems and provide clarity in the realm of love relationships.

Still, it takes truth-telling and consistent practice. I had a friend who said she would always choose to have some therapy in a relationship. She said,

"I'll never be in another unsupervised relationship again."

She and her partner had started therapy, and it was a tribute to the supervision of a guide, a healing companion for our psychological selves.

I'm amazed that anyone gets along! When you think of idiosyncracies, unconscious projections, restimulations from the past, and the relationship history of your partner, it's stunning that love works.

My history involves: married men, violent men, liars, con artists, the immature, the "not ready," the lost, the desperate, and the users.

* I've also been most of these myself at different points.

Women are often the adaptors. They mold and change to fit a relationship. We need to question our needs and desires, and ask questions like:

- What does support feel/look like to me?
- What is a conscious relationship, and am I in one?
- Is my partner committed to communicating and working with emotional stuff?
- Does my partner want to be in a relationship?
- Do I?

Women also are initiators. Let's initiate growing, healthy, fun love relationships.

record
Book
of
Wrongs

"Love keeps no record of wrongs."

Apostle Paul

Living the process

I had a friend who talked about "real love stories" which is the stuff you don't hear about during the romance phase.

It's where you go on a long trip and he splashes gasoline on your shoe and whistles too loudly.

It's where she never wants to hear whistling and complains that your shoes are squeaking on the gas pedal.

It's finding out what lies beneath the fights and skirmishes of daily living. What are you really fighting about?

It's figuring out a mutual language, developing trust, increasing intimacy, telling the truth microscopically, and revealing yourself deeply.

It's about being exposed as who you really are.

WHO is THAT?

It is being independent, interdependent, and dependent.

It's about building a best friend·ship with your lover.

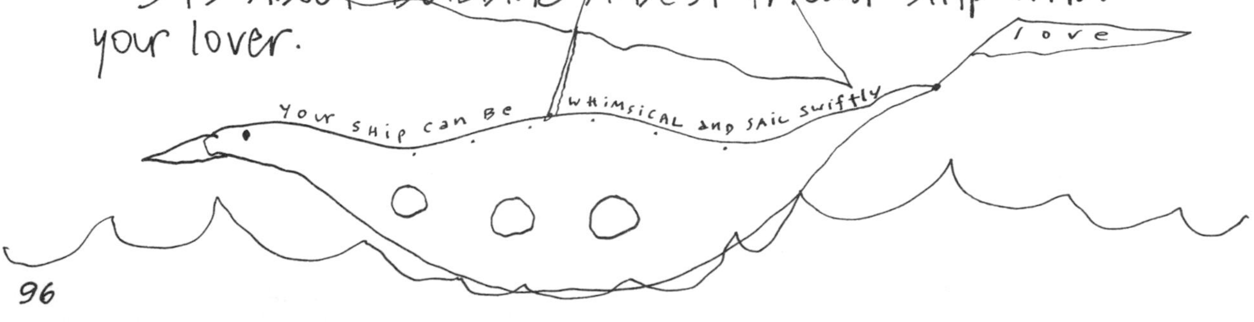
love
your ship can be whimsical and sail swiftly

It's about asking for what you need or want, regardless of the outcome.

I often see women settle for less because they're afraid of loss, lonely, needy, or having great sex.

The process of love is messy, holy, ordinary, and wildly hope-full.

Your heart will be very involved

Tell your loved one:

- What you truly feel
- Who you really are
- What you really want
- How to love you best
- How to listen to you

As women, we deserve to be fully met, deeply loved, and equally at play in the process of loving.

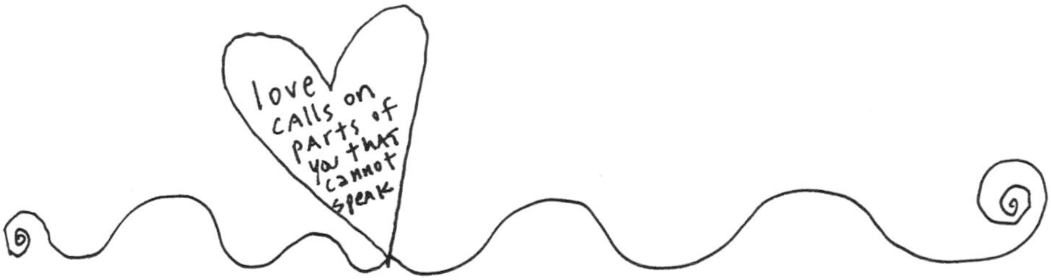
love calls on parts of you that cannot speak

"Love as a power can go anywhere. It isn't sentimental. It doesn't have to be pretty, yet it doesn't deny pain."

Sharon Salzberg

Motherhood

In childhood, we play dolls, simulate births, and pretend to be mommies. Then we gradually find out that we can actually *be* mommies.

When I was 11, my mother told my brother and I that she was expecting — on April Fool's Day. She was 41 and it didn't seem likely, so we laughed.

My brother, Andrew, was born in September 1965 and I was the happiest big sister ever. *I* got to practice being a mom and I loved it.

I still tell people that I used to change his diaper, and at 31 years old he answers, "Not recently."

I terminated 3 pregnancies in my 20's because I felt there was no other way. I wish I had been ready. It is one of my greatest dreams and biggest fears to become a mother. I think it is the bravest human act to become a parent.

I watch my friend Adrienne, who soars as a mother. She is more open, allowing, and full of love than before. She turned to me in the delivery room after giving birth and said,

"Susan, this is *Big Love*."

Zoe
Arielle
is Gorgeous

Zoe is my godchild, and I marvel at her perfection. She is a teacher for me. Motherhood is a sacred trust, a holy act, and a trip of surrender.

Whenever we give birth, adopt, or act as temporary mothers, we have this maternal gift, this nurturing ability, and it is divine.

We are all mothers in special ways. Godmothers, big sisters, aunts, or simply friends with children. There are so many children already here who need love — it isn't necessary to be a mother to experience mothering.

children are our teachers and healers

"Women without children are also the best of mothers, often, with the patience, interest and saving grace that the constant relationship with children cannot always sustain. I come to crave our talk and our children gain precious aunts. Women who are not mothering their own children have the clarity and focus to see deeply into the character of children webbed by family. A child is fortunate who feels witnessed as a person outside relationships with parents, by another adult."

Louise Erdrich, The Blue Jay's Dance

"Having a child is like growing another heart."

Rosie O'Donnell

Hopes

Through all the relationships, we keep hoping we'll be fully met by someone fabulous.

"Hope is the thing with feathers that perches in the soul, and sings the tunes without words and never stops at all."

Emily Dickinson

Hope keeps us answering personal ads, going on blind dates, meeting our friends' friends, or being set up by relatives. WHAT is she/he like?

Even when we are satisfied, and happily alone, we entertain hopes once in awhile during romantic movies, or holidays, or when we're sick. Hoping for a marvelous union is not wrong. Hope is a great companion and motivator. Even when I had stopped looking for a partner, a tiny part of me still hoped...

When friends, Roy and Vanessa said, "He's the male version of you." I resisted.

He couldn't be all that they said. Could he?

He was.

SARK's
Journal
and
Play! Book

We met at a party for my third book, on Oct 23, 1993. I was wearing a short black dress and glowing neon eye on my chest. The initial feeling between us was so strong that we acted very uncharacteristically and avoided each other for the rest of the party, and didn't talk for 4 months after that.

He lived in Los Angeles, and I had vowed to never again go out with someone who didn't live in the same city.

I saw him again at a brunch in his honor. He was wearing a purple jacket, smiling, and I had the same strong feeling as the first time we met. At brunch, I played a game by asking everyone at the table if they sleep neat or messy. I asked, "What does your bed look like when you get out of it?"

He said, "Neither neat nor messy. You just know that a dance has taken place."

There was butcher paper and crayons at our table, and he began drawing a portrait on his placemat. I looked over and noticed that he was using all the colors that I never touch—the golds, browns, olive greens.

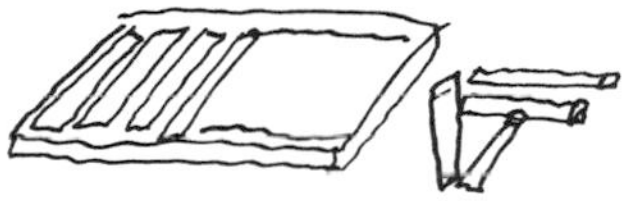

Then I thought suddenly, "This is the man I'm going to marry."

I had never thought I'd marry anyone and used to laugh at people who "suddenly knew" about marriage. stupid romantic idiots.

Then I realized that his colors complemented mine.

I primarily use primary colors.

We made arrangements to have tea the next day. A few hours before, I asked my assistant to cancel. I felt so skeptical and terrified. I thought, "This isn't even a date. He lives in Los Angeles. His name is Craig. Why bother."

He had already checked out of his hotel and so it wasn't possible to cancel!

Then he sent a fax.

SARK
&
McNAIR
at FOUR
at the
Ritz
Can't Wait!
CMcNair

When I saw it, I knew I needed to meet him. Suddenly I became 13 years old, and couldn't decide what to wear. I tried on about 16 outfits before rushing off to the Ritz, 1/2 hour early, so I could get the best table.

When I arrived, he was already sitting there, waiting for the best table!

Within 2 hours, we were discussing our marriage, crying together, and laughing at each other's stories.

When I voiced my strong concerns about his living in Los Angeles, he said,

"Susan, real love moves."

This touched me deeply until I realized that he might expect me to move to Los Angeles! He said, "Susan, I will move to San Francisco."

So, in August 1996, he sold his house and is moving to San Francisco! (He moved. He's here now.)

And the love and learning continues...

I like to introduce him as "the man of my dreams—and my nightmares."

I couldn't have hoped for someone so wonderful, or that I was this wonderful.

Love inspires hope.

I am awed by hope.

Love and Romance

Down in the GARDEN By anne GEDDES
I Will leAve you never By HUGH & GAyle Prather
operating instructions By anne LAMOTT
Two PART invention By MADeleine L'engle
centering and the ART of intiMACY By GAY Hendricks, PH.D. and KAthLyn Hendricks, PH.D.
embracing our selves By HAL Stone, PH.D & SiDrA winkelman stone PH.D
Secrets of A very GOOD MArriAGe By SHerry Suib Cohen
embracing the Beloved By stephen and ondrea Levine
conscious Loving By GAY Hendricks PH.D and KAthLyn Hendricks PH.D
Getting the love you want By HArville Hendrix
How They Met By nancy COBB
Temporarily out of print
The Blue JAY's Dance By Louise erdrich
Time-out For Parents By CHeri Huber and MeLinDA Guyol, MFCC
The women's comfort Book by Jennifer Louden
SOUL MATES By THOMAS Moore
The Heart of MArriAGe By cathleen rountree

Music

- THe Dreamer, romances for the Alto Flute, VOL. 2 By Michael Hoppé and Tim Wheater
- THe postman (il postino) Composed, orchestrated and conducted By Luis Bacalov

Movie

- enchanted April

Terror of Cellulite

Here's what I've done to try and eradicate cellulite:

- ridden a bicycle 3,000 miles 
  (and I still had cellulite at the end of it!)
- endured a 2-year cellulite massage program
  (intensely painful, very expensive.)
- ran 14 miles a week compulsively
  (I also ate so little that I nearly fell asleep while running.)
- Tried creams, loofah scrubs, steam heat and "wraps". 
  miracle cream
  (these worked for about 6 hours.)

Still, cellulite creeps back. Would it bother me if I couldn't see it? Why is it so unsightly, and why do I care?

Perhaps I see it as a flaw, or evidence of pain, or being out of control, not in shape.

Women can be relentlessly focused on matters of appearance.

I remember my first sighting of cellulite. I was a college freshman and had spent the first year eating donuts. I was trying on bathing suits, and caught a rear view in the changing room mirror...

so many donuts

The Horror of cellulite!

I've spent inordinate amounts of time arranging my thigh fat while lying down in the sun, so that no cellulite shows, or backing away from a lover so he doesn't see the backs of my legs.

so much hiding

Now I eat chocolate, drink red wine, and make feeble attempts to accept my cellulite. Failing that, I'd just like to sit in a lawn chair in a pair of shorts without adjusting my thighs so there are no fat bulges.

Madness! I see these obsessive thoughts and marvel at my mind's ability to try and make it "normal."

My friend had a new lover, and began backing out of the room after sex, and all of a sudden stopped and said intensely, "These are my thighs. I have cellulite. Take it or leave it."

Her lover replied, "What's cellulite?"

Let's laugh at cellulite! Start a cellulite acceptance club. Find ways to make friends with it. I realize that cellulite has stuck by me all these years—it must have something to offer.

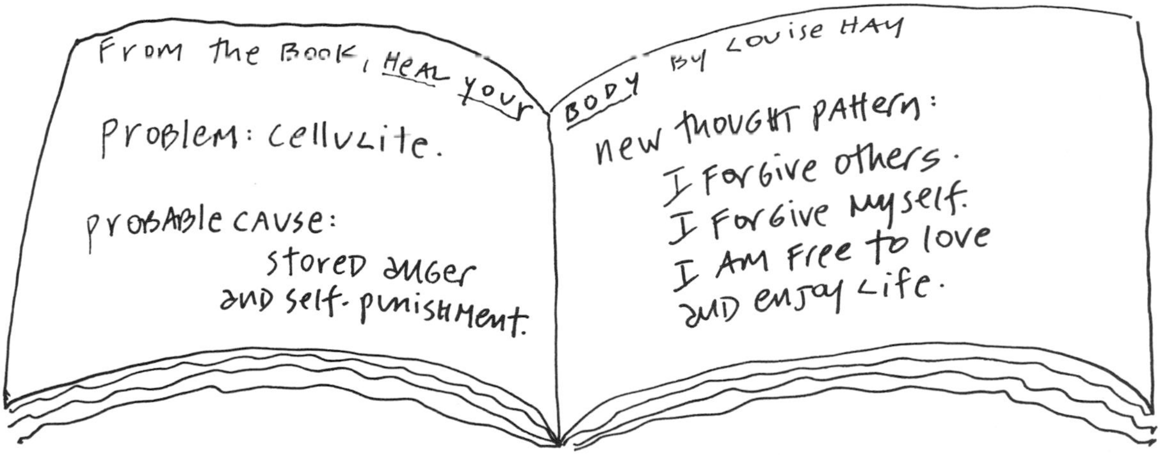
From the book, Heal Your Body by Louise Hay
Problem: cellulite.
Probable cause:
stored anger and self-punishment.
New thought pattern:
I forgive others.
I forgive myself.
I am free to love and enjoy life.

I also think that if we could get cellulite put onto Barbie dolls, it would help a lot with self-acceptance.

Tyranny of Size

I remember being described as a "big girl" as a teenager, and to me, this meant FAT. One time, I was rejected by a dance teacher who told me I was "too heavy" to take ballet.

Perhaps he was terrified of loud, actual-sized women.

Women are tyrannized by size. Sizes of clothes can haunt you. I wear everything from size 8–16. When I find something that fits me in a size 16, I feel like a huge tank. I have cut size tags out of clothes.

S
M
L
XL

Size of body parts is also an ever-present awareness. For instance, I have small feet, which for women is considered dainty, feminine, and somehow pleasing. My friend Susan had size 9 feet at 12 years old and was told her feet were the size of boats.

She walked with her toes curled trying to disguise this. Big hair is considered good. Big legs, bad. Big bottom: worst of all.

I used to slam my hip against a wall to try and make it smaller. I started weight training mostly to make my butt smaller.

One time I was walking up the stairs in front of a lover, and he said, "You really do have a big butt!" I was devastated.

Sometimes I feel that my body is turning into a couch. Padded arms, big plump cushions, and even tiny uncomfortable pillows along the backside.

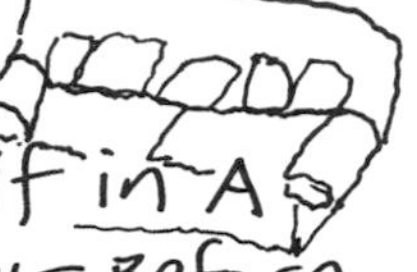

I continue to eat like an angry child—as if in a food trance—I repeat what made me sick the night before.

I feel horrified by the expansion of my flesh, ashamed that it matters to me so much, and defiant that I do not feel comfortable in my body.

So often I am paralyzed inside my body and barely notice its boundaries and edges. During sex, or trying to zip up a too-small skirt, or in a bathing suit, I become acutely aware of my physical self.

I am drawn to dance, to swing on the trapeze, to swim and run. I notice that I hide from these activities if I am feeling "too heavy" which is often a complete distortion of my actual size. There are also times I fall silent, my body critic numbed into some kind of peace treaty.

the white flag

Somehow as women, we connect our various sizes to our self-worth. We have mental images of ideal sizes—even if it's not in our heritage to be that way.

We know that men appreciate actual-sized women—and that other women struggle with this issue—yet we wish we could be smaller.

We want to shrink ourselves

We compliment weight loss, monitor our appetites, and shrink ourselves to fit some kind of standard. I wish we could all be the size we actually are. One size doesn't fit all—because there are as many sizes as there are women.

Let's look closer at the size of our hearts, the width of our souls, and the length of our spirits.

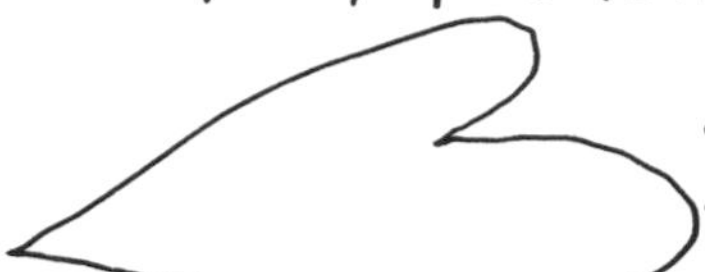

let your heart grow in size

"Phenomenal Woman" by Maya Angelou

Pretty women wonder where my secret lies.
I'm not cute or built to suit a fashion model's size
But when I start to tell them,
They think I'm telling lies.
I say,
It's in the reach of my arms,
The span of my hips,
The stride of my step,
The curl of my lips.
I'm a woman
Phenomenally.
Phenomenal woman,
That's me.

This is an excerpt from her fabulous poem. Read all of Maya Angelou's poetry.

Importance of Breasts

"Large breasts are like pets. Everyone likes them, but you're the one who has to take care of them."
SARK

I had large breasts at age 12. Nobody explained where they came from, and I longed for the days when I played basketball with the guys, without a shirt.

I quickly learned to manipulate men with my breasts. (Also known as honkers, hooters, bazooms, headlights, tits, boobies, and just plain big tits). I wore tiny tube tops, halter tops, too-small t-shirts, and sucked in my stomach so my breasts would look even larger. I learned that men stared at my chest when we talked. I began saying, "Stop staring at my breasts. My eyes are up here."

I did the "pencil test" where if a pencil stays under your breast, you have big breasts. I could wear 2 pencils all day.

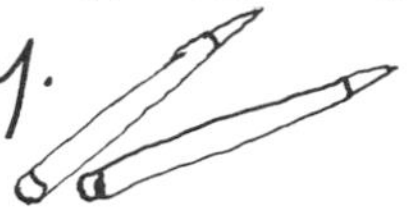

Women with smaller breasts seemed so lucky to me. I dreamed of running without a shelf of flesh moving up and down.

Everything I read promoted either the sexual or maternal nature of breasts

In my school, girls with big breasts were automatic sluts.

I saw my grandmother without a blouse one time. She had had breast cancer and was very matter of fact about showing me her chest. There was a long tight scar and I remember envying what seemed like freedom to me.

I grew bored with men's preoccupation with breasts, even though I still relied on their "power."

During my 30's, I began worrying about sagging breasts, and began wearing oversize shirts to try and hide from any scrutiny. I also developed posture problems from slumping down in an attempt to make my chest look smaller.

What is this obsession with cleavage?

I can appreciate the little tunnel made where breasts are pushed together, but it gets sweaty. You can keep things in there— money, perfume, or a phone number, and it's great for softening the butter at fancy restaurants. Men get delirious at the sight of cleavage (some women too). I think they imagine living in there. Just curling up between the breasts like giant soft pillows. Pillows with nipples.

"I used to be good at limbo until I grew breasts."

SARK

I dream of a time where women stand proud and tall— whatever their breast size. Where breasts are not objectified, but just welcomed and healthy. Where all of us are satisfied with our breasts and their size.

RADICAL SELF-ACCEPTANCE

Someone called my inspiration phone line and left this message: 

"SARK, I send you waking naps, where for brief periods of time, you can stop working on yourself, and simply luxuriate in where you are right now, just as you are."

I felt my shoulders come down about a foot and breathed deeply. All of a sudden, I saw this

incessant pattern of working and pushing

My boyfriend says he feels like sometimes we work on our relationship more than we actually just live in it.

Women are often immersed in renovation—of deep psychological explorations, long processing talks, relationship work, the heaving around of emotional boulders.

Abandonment
Hyper-sensitivity
neediness

Whenever I hear the term self-acceptance, I usually think, "Yeah, after I lose that weight, improve the cellulite, trim those thighs, meditate more often, be more fun to be with."

I propose a new way.

RADICAL SELF-ACCEPTANCE

Do not stand naked in front of your mirror and accept what you see.

Wear large pajamas and stay in bed all day and night.

Buy or Borrow self-improvement Books, But Don't read them. Stack them Around your Bedroom and use them As places to rest Bowls of cookies.

WATCH exercise shows on television, But Don't Do the exercises. Practice Believing that the Benefit lies in imagining yourself Doing the exercises.

Don't power WALK. Saunter slowly in the sun, eating chocolate, and carry A Blanket so you can take A nap.

SOFT NAP Blanket

Stop looking At cellucite. Only view your Body From the angles that Don't show it.

never use A scale. If your clothes keep Fitting, you weigh the same. (Although it Doesn't really fit into radical self-Acceptance, I Feel compelled to Add A cautionary note From elizabeth Taylor—"Beware of elastic waisted pants! you can get quite FAT without realizing it.") THIS HAS HAppened to me.

Simply luxuriate in where you Are right now.

read this. Breathe. Adopt this PHILOSOPHY of course you might Begin new exercise plans, meditate more often... BLAH, BlAH, BlAH.

But where Are you right now?

Without our flaws, faults, and foibles, we would be less lovable— much less lovable.

Treat yourself as kindly as you do your best friend

How kind and understanding we are when we help a friend in crisis, or just in a low spot.

Friend in a low spot

Drench yourself in self-kindness!

Women are very good at shining kindness outward, yet if you ask how kind they are to themselves, they often cry.

Turn the kindness spotlight inward.

Before we can move to healthier ways, we must be where we actually are.

Radical self-acceptance is a connecting, soft, slow, and compassionate way of being. We can help each other.

When you see your "sister" beating up on herself, take her weapons away and just hold her.

When you watch animals, you see only self-acceptance. Find ways to expand radical self-acceptance in your life. Adopt a friend and exchange stories of self-acceptance. So often, we trade stories of how bad we've been, or are.

Shift the focus.

Describe the ways you learned to accept yourself today—or last week.

I myself, live under siege from the inner critic, the judge, and the "pusher." I'm studying these selves of my personality and giving them new jobs. FAR AWAY

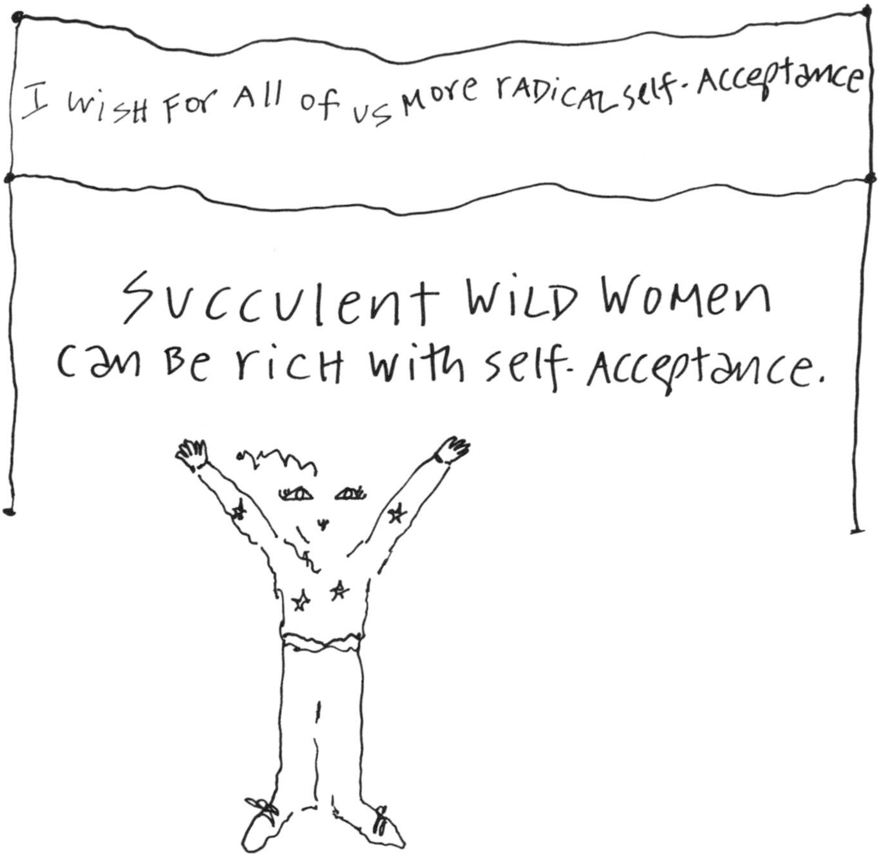
I wish for all of us more radical self-acceptance
Succulent Wild Women can be rich with self-acceptance.

Nourishment from the inside

Let us as women be thankful for hearty appetites! Allow us to feel true hunger.

I see so much self-imposed starvation among women— myself included. and then we hide away and eat our hearts out....

The language of cake:

"Oh just a tiny slice!"
"Please— the smallest slice you can cut."
"I'm being so bad!"

Or, a marvelous woman I met, who said:

"I eat cake for breakfast. I know I'm going to want it all day anyway, so I just start with it."
Michelle

Don't we deserve to eat?

How do you nourish yourself? (Besides food)

nourishing touch?

nourishing walks?

nourishing books?

You
Are
The
Book

nourishing words?

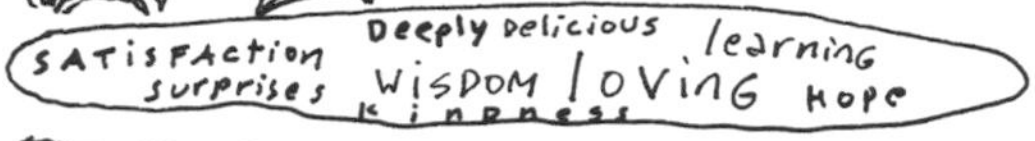
SATISFACTION
surprises
Deeply Delicious
WISDOM
loving
Kindness
learning
Hope

nourishing naps?

nourishing self-talk? you are so deeply loved

The nourishment starts on the inside. When we tell ourselves and others the truth and identify what we really want and need, we are nourishing ourselves.

Satisfy your hungers for:

- Spirituality what does yours look like?
- intimate connection How does it feel?
- creative expression Are you free?
- physical movement can you move?
- conscious breathing let breath heal you
- Being of service How?

Women are often nourishing others, and need to practice more self-nourishment.

Keep taking your inner nourishment pulse. Notice the tendency to leave your self.

How is your inside nourishment?

How does it look inside you?

WHAT MAGAZINES TELL US

- THAT SIZE 12 IS BIG.
- THAT WE MUST DRESS RIGHT, OR END UP IN A "DON'T" COLUMN.
- THAT WE MUST CONSTANTLY SEEK PERFECTION.
- THE SAME INFORMATION EVERY MONTH WITH DIFFERENT TITLES.
- HOW TO COOK, EAT, DRESS, BEHAVE, AND THINK.

I READ 50-60 MAGAZINES EVERY MONTH. MANY OF THESE ARE "WOMEN'S MAGAZINES." THERE IS AN ASTONISHING AMOUNT OF INFORMATION IN THESE MAGAZINES. SOME OF IT IS INFORMATIVE, SUPPORTIVE, AND REVEALING. MUCH OF IT IS REPETITIVE, NEGATIVE, AND DEMEANING.

I READ MAGAZINES PARTLY TO FEEL CONNECTED TO OTHER WOMEN. WHEN I READ THE LETTERS TO THE EDITORS, I FEEL LIKE I KNOW THESE WOMEN, THAT WE'RE ON THE SAME WAVELENGTH.

ADVENTUROUS LIFE
NON CONFORMIST
INSPIRATION GUIDE TO LIFE
CELEBRATION OF DIFFERENCES

"MAGAZINES" THAT FLOAT AROUND IN MY MIND

SOME OF WHAT I READ IN MAGAZINES FEEDS MY INNER CRITIC: I HAVEN'T REDUCED MY THIGHS, SHRUNK MY DRESS SIZE, OR STOPPED SNACKING BETWEEN MEALS.

I want magazines to be more intimate, braver, and more collaborative. Many are moving in this direction.

Magazines rely on their readers to buy and subscribe—let's tell them what we want to see!

- More actual-sized bodies
- First person accounts
- Being more creatively alive resources
- Celebration of women as they really are

The magazines are only reflecting what we don't tell them.

Let's send e-mail, letters, and make phone calls to suggest, offer, and constructively complain. Let's fill the pages with our real selves and faults!

We must remember that magazines are skewed by the "formula." They do not reflect our truth!

Sage Woman
Lotus
Transformation
intuition
Yoga Journal
Common Boundary
Shambhala
New Age Journal
Utne Reader
The Sun
New Moon

Some magazines that nourish me

FAT

Appetites By Geneen Roth
Getting Our Bodies Back By Christine Caldwell
Feeding the Hungry Heart By Geneen Roth
Staying Healthy with Nutrition By Elson Haas M.D.
Nothing to Lose By Cheri Erdman
The Owl Was a Baker's Daughter By Marion Woodman
Real Gorgeous By Kaz Cooke
When Food is Love By Geneen Roth
Enlightened Eating By Rebecca Ruggles Radcliffe
The Woman's Comfort Book By Jennifer Louden
The Invisible Woman Confronting Weight Prejudice in America By Charisse Goodman
Intuitive Eating By Evelyn Tribole Elyse Resch
Breaking Free From Compulsive Eating By Geneen Roth

resource

- "Radiance" A Magazine for larger women. To order call 510·482·0680 or write: PO Box 30246, Oakland, CA 94604. $20 (U.S.) and $26 (Canada) for a quarterly subscription

Music

- Been Found by Ashford and Simpson with Maya Angelou
- Endless Waves, Vol 1 by Gabrielle Roth

Journaling

Journals can provide a pathway to the inner you

Every woman is living a journey of her own life. We are each teachers and healers, and our voices count.

"In our journals we are in search of the real self—of what really moves us, what we really think, what we really feel."

Elizabeth O'Connor

The blank page calls us out to play with pens, paints, glue, lipstick, ink or pencils.

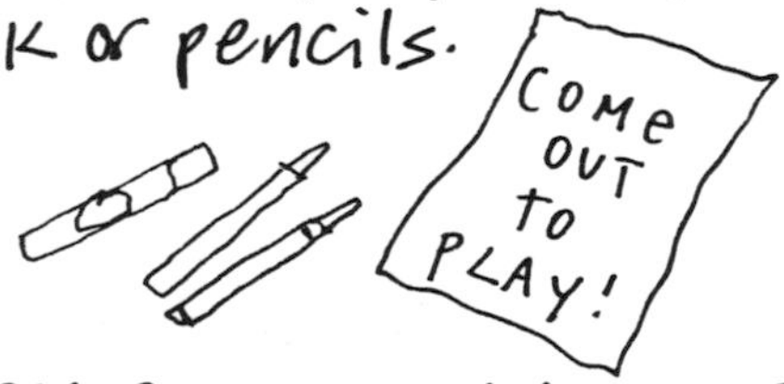
COME
OUT
TO
PLAY!

The journal is a witness, an unconditional friend, a soul teacher. Sometimes, we just complain. Writing out the dark thoughts lessens their power. Having conversations with ourselves in journals gives us chances to work things out in private. We collect and form our own history (and herstory) with journals.

I started keeping journals in 1979. The hundreds of volumes are precious to me, and are full of my life and lives.

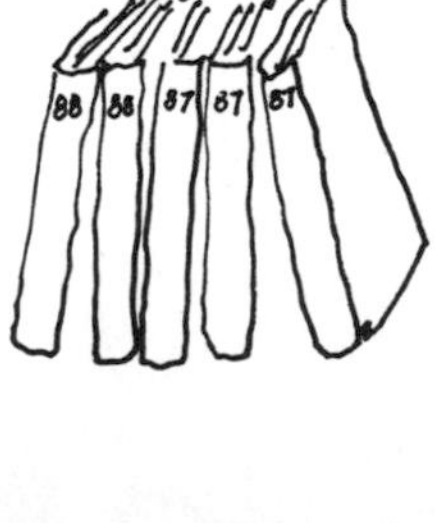
88
88
87
87
87

Now that I write books, I write in my journal less often. I've stopped judging the quantity of my writing.

For a long time, journals were my only "proof" that I could write.

The Proving Journal

People would ask what I did, and I would say, "I'm a writer!" They inevitably would ask, "What do you write?"

When I answered "journals,"

the precious journal

sometimes they chuckled or smirked, or said, "No really—what do you write—for real?" As though journals were less valuable somehow.

Journals are not less valuable

Whatever coaxes us out of hiding, to write, record, and express, is a revolutionary act. It says that we believe our lives count. Our lives do count.

I will Always Be thank-full to: Maya angelou, anaïs Nin, anne Morrow Lindbergh, May Sarton, Colette, Gertrude Stein, and so many other great writers, for opening up their journals, and their lives, to me.

It gave me courage to write my own journals and books.

THANK YOU.

When I look back in those journals now, I see clearly that nothing is lost. I'm using words and images from those journals in my current writings.

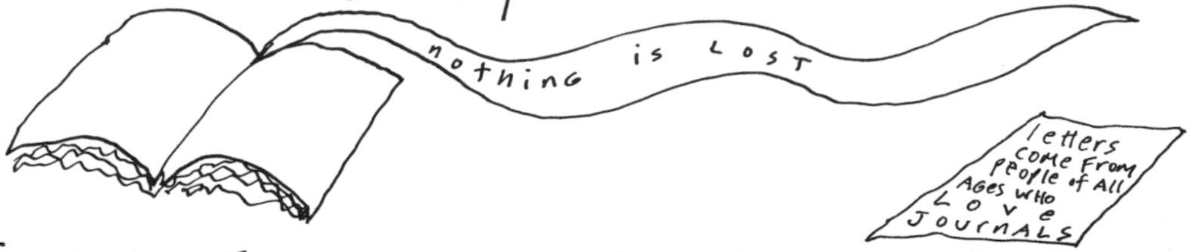
nothing is lost
letters come from people of all ages who love journals

In 1993, I created SARK's Journal and Play! Book as sort of a journal guidebook and actual journal. I get letters from 8-year-old girls who are filling these journal pages with their list of "I wants" and describing who they love and why. It fills my heart to think of young women and girls playing on

B i g B l a n k P A G e s

Instead of being trapped in Barbie pink plastic diaries with locks—as though they have to keep their thoughts locked up.

Before

I want:
now

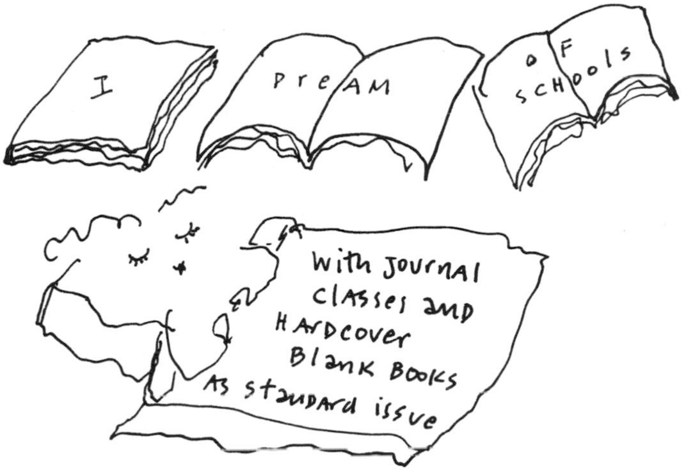
I
Dream
of
schools
with journal classes and hardcover blank books as standard issue

It doesn't matter what you write in a journal. It matters that it is *yours*.

"I began these pages for myself, in order to think out my own particular pattern of living, my own individual balance of life, work, and human relationships."

Anne Morrow Lindbergh

YOU

Your own journal awaits you.

Jump.

WAYS TO BEGIN A JOURNAL

the smile book
captivating moments

Get a blank book, lined book, one with quotes or pictures — whatever makes you smile inside and want to rush home to write in it.

Take your book and make it yours with photos, dots, scribbles, or just your name (or secret name).

Carefully choose your writing tools so that your words can gleefully leap onto the paper.

I feel so out of control and lost. Still, I laugh...

Begin writing about anything: the branch of a tree, a kind cotton sock, your cat's paw, a piece of neglected fruit, the way you curl into sleep, a prayer for your unborn child, what you wish you could say, what love looks like, your wish for the world, the love life of flies, what kind of flowers make you gasp.

let your pages be ordinary
and human and exquisitely you

Read Julia Cameron, Natalie Goldberg, May Sarton, Anne Morrow Lindbergh, Anaïs Nin — there are so many great women writers waiting for you to read them.

Let your journal be a joy for you.

Story·telling

Women tell stories to each other.

We sit or walk close together, telling stories of our lives, loves, discoveries, challenges, pains, and dreams.

stories pass through us like streams...

Or, as my friend Susan says: "Wasn't it grand to talk about everything—and nothing?"

We can talk on the phone for hours about nothing in particular

Stories are our way to illuminate the path and find common ground.

Our illusions of separation disappear when we hear stories of another's struggles or discoveries.

We hear ourselves say,

"I can relate to that!"

in our stories are seeds of our deepest longings and wishes. Through story, creative buds can burst into life.

Books are collections of stories for everyone to read and find their own meaning in. My books tell stories of my life and process. I believe these stories assist people in their creative growth. especially women.

A story can travel without you and inspire many

"every word a woman writes changes the story of the world, revises the official version."

Carolyn See

My story of sitting in a hotel lobby with a sign that read

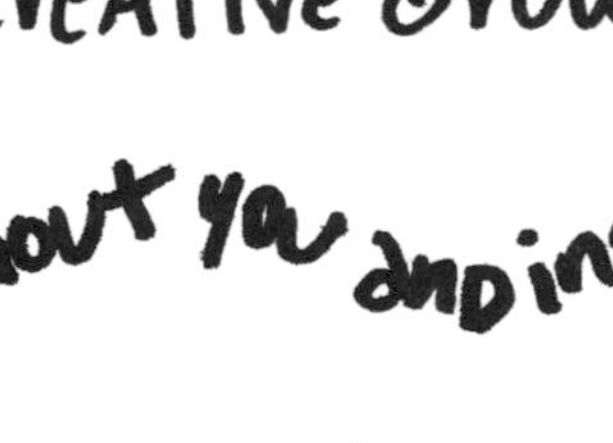
Artist
Available
for Dinner

has inspired other women to venture out into the world more creatively or unusually.

My story of placing an AD that said:

incredible housesitter seeks incredible house

which resulted in a rent-free mansion for 2 years, encouraged other women to place ads or reach out in new ways.

When I found my magic cottage in San Francisco by visualizing it and describing it in my journal, it prompted others to visualize more.

There are many types of magic cottages

All the stories I had read or heard about these subjects inspired me—which resulted in my experimenting, and then writing about my experiences. Whatever inspires **you** will inspire others!

We are richly connected by our stories

Telling stories through letters, journals, books, by computer, or on the phone are all ways to connect with other creative souls.

Don't forget your dream life!

Tell More stories!

Your stories can teach, uplift, remind, give permission, reassure, inspire, give strength, allow humor.

The tiniest story in your life can deeply touch another.
You cannot know the effect your story might have.

please let your stories be heard

"A story is a medicine that greases and hoists the pulleys, shows us the way out, down, in and around, cuts for us fine wide doors in previously blank walls, doors which lead us to our own knowing."

Clarissa Pinkola Estés

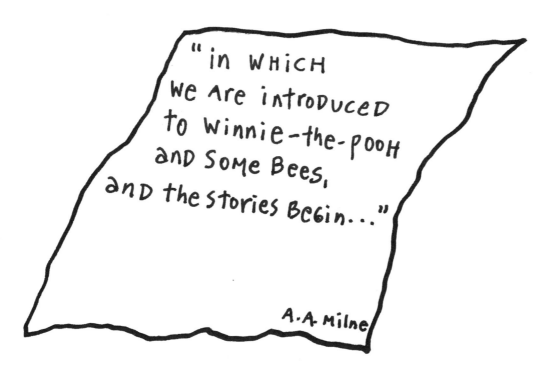

"in which
we are introduced
to Winnie-the-Pooh
and some Bees,
and the stories begin..."

A.A. Milne

Painting

Painting is putting colors from your heart onto paper. Painting is playing with color. Painting is dancing on

paper

Truth: we need more women to be painting.

So often, we don't try new forms for fear that it "won't look good." I myself have produced some of the ugliest paintings ever! Hideous, rust-colored, unidentifiable blobs, that I hurriedly threw away.

It is so easy to let our inner critic stand over us as we paint, and chortle at our feeble results. Even before the paint dries, the critic judges it inferior. Many of us don't even try to paint!

We wonder if we're a painter—and if we don't see evidence of prodigy at a young age, or hear an inner calling, we conclude we're not painters. Also, who are our female role models? Truth: We can all paint.

Perhaps not "professionally" (unless we want to) but think of all that you do that may not be "professional": cooking, photography, running...

You can express parts of yourself in painting that come from nowhere else. There is an interior part of you that has no words and dreams in color.

It is the part that gasps at sunset sky colors, pauses at a pine tree glistening with dew, and sees the sunlight on a child's hair.

HOW TO paint

Put your ego, critic, JUDGE in A Drawer.
lock it.
Go on an Art store Adventure. Buy smooth or nubbly paper—whatever sings to your Fingers.
Tear it into ODD-sized pieces. Buy one Brush.
Choose colors that you love in ink, watercolor, Acrylic, oil or **Finger paints.**
Mix colors randomly or put Directly onto paper.
experiment. **Keep Going.** Make more mistakes.
LAUGH AT WHAT Develops. **put layers of color on top of each other.** Tear the paper up if you Don't like it.
Glue the pieces into the center of the next picture. See if it Develops into anything.
Spill paint onto the paper. WATCH WHAT forms next. This is painting.
You Are A painter.

Perhaps your painting calls for photographs, or tiny doors cut to open, or bits of flowers. Maybe it wants to be a card for your dearest friend, or a page in your journal.

The paint will lead you to new places if you can follow the splashes.

Where do the splashes lead?

Be kind to your new paint spirits— they might be young and unknown. How will you know about yourself and painting if you don't paint? Certainly not from past evidence. That has no basis. Did someone tell you you can't paint? A person, or your own inner critic?

They lie.

Paint your heart's colors!
let paint leap out.

Allow your inner visions to be in color

Costumes

Succulent Wild Women wear costumes.

Costumes can be:

Outrageous hats

painted gloves

and slippers

Velvet capes

Vintage jackets with rare buttons

Decorated handbags

unusual shoes

HANDMADE JEWELRY

Pieces OF BATIK

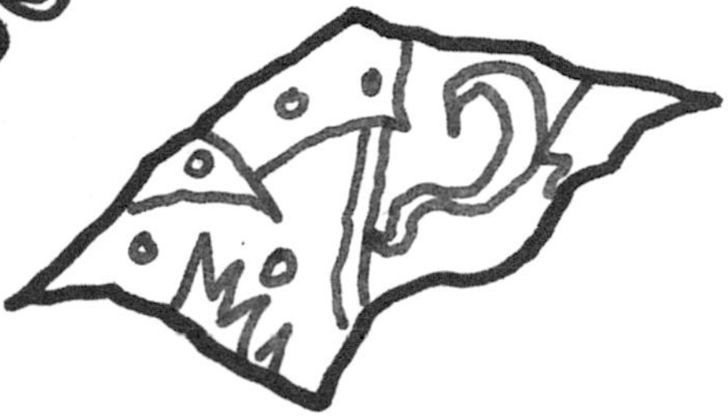

painted silk scarves

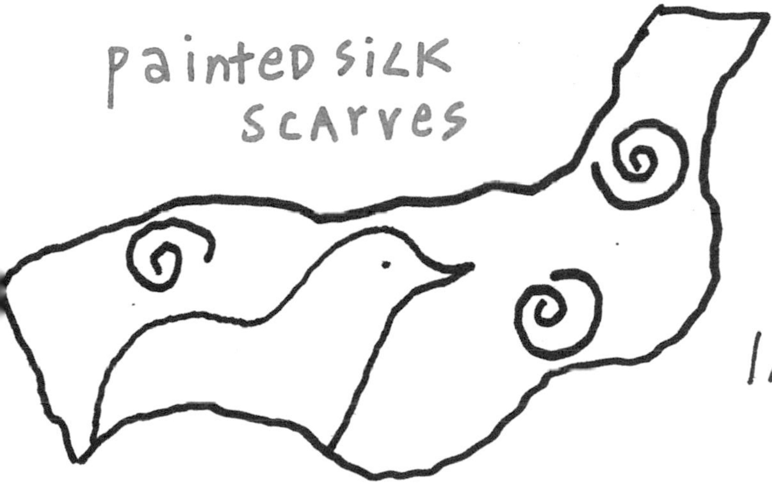

large color-full rings

Wearable toys, tiaras and necklaces made of symbols.

Costumes are a way for women to play adult dress up — we can let different parts of our personalities out to have fun.

One time, I was traveling in Mendocino—A romantic California coastal town—and saw a rare sight:

Six women on the street, all wearing plastic Groucho Marx glasses, noses, and hats.

I stopped to applaud them, and found out they were 4 generations of women, playing together on vacation. I declared them to be succulent wild women, and the great-grandmother threw her hat in the air and said,

"You betcha, Honey!" 

They hustled off down the street, arm in arm. We forget to dress in bright colors, in our own distinctive styles.

WHAT will the neighbors think?

They'll think that they wish they could have fun too. Ask them! We must wrap ourselves like the gifts that we are.

Costumes promote adventures. I used to go out in the Bahamas, in an evening dress, riding a bicycle and carrying a bamboo walking stick. Then, I'd parade through the casino carrying my stick. You cannot be lonely this way.

Costumes are according to mood. Take your temperature before going out (or staying in). What do you really want to wear?

WHAT speaks of your soul?

Sometimes a costume is a favorite cotton shirt and pants — I have one top I call my nanny top — because that's what I feel like when I wear it.

My most common costume is pajamas. I like white cotton men's, with drawstring pants. size XL for room to dance!

I paint my jackets and shoes when they begin to bore me. Sometimes I ruin them by painted "mistakes." These I cut up and turn into collages (or sometimes I just throw them away!).

I'd like to expand my costume wearing as I age. Let's all wear bright togas, wild shoes, flabbergasting hats and meet in a drumming circle, in a forest near a hot spring. All costumes welcome!

How to arrange a Succulent Wild Woman evening:

Poster size
Succulent
Wild Women
Do wild things!
Meet us for an
evening of delicious
food, abundant
laughter,
poetry,
and inspiration.

or  really tiny

Send an invitation of unusual size and words.
include poetry.

"extend surprising invitations."
SARK

Make your invitation succulent.

Describe events briefly and with intrigue:

"Imagination Festival with other Succulent Wild Women, we want you!"

Dress: Wild imaginings, Dancing shoes.

Food: Chocolate, fruit, homemade bread, cheese.

Purpose: To be succulent together!

Arrange to do one activity: (or more if the spirits move you!)

- Dancing at home, in a wild club you would normally not go to, in a smoke-free, wood-floored dance studio.
- Drumming at a beach by a fire, by candlelight at home, in a forest by moon-light.
- Poetry reading in a circle randomly, in a garden, at dawn.
- Journal writing spend time writing together about: love, radiance, yearnings, travel, adventure, or serendipity. Read excerpts to each other.

There are so many succulent ways to connect with women. We are all craving unusual, inspiring, soulful times.

let's spend
more of our lives
in the
soulful times

MAKING MISTAKES

Creativity is filled with "mistakes." Women are often preoccupied with perfection and miss out on the mistake-making process. We start with a vision in our imagination—then we try to translate it into paint, clay, crayon, pastel, dance or song.

The paint leaps off the brush and a big dot appears on the paper. Is it a mistake? or a messenger of color, sent to invite us to explore?

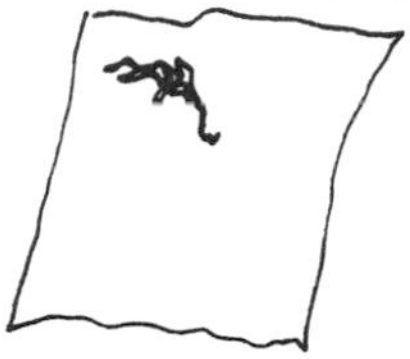

So often, I scribble or color and then judge the result too quickly. I decide it is inferior, or a mistake, or not worthy in some way. Yet the process is a glory if I can detach from the result.

Sometimes while writing a book, I imagine an audience of critics looking scornfully at what I'm writing. I call in my creative and spiritual mentors to "scatter the crowd" and restore some balance.

We need to make more mistakes! As women, and people, and especially creatively. Start more projects! Start more than you can ever finish. Fill yourself overly full so that your imagination spills out. Watch children. So much of what they do is a "mistake" by our narrow adult standards. Women can step boldly forward as <u>working creative people</u>—not just hobbyists, dabblers, and <u>only</u> dreamers.

There is a marvelous organization called Guerilla Girls—they wear masks and appear at museums and art openings to expose the small percentage of women artists showing in museums, and other injustices for women in the art world. In order to have our creative voice heard, we must speak—even if we are unsure about what to say. Dare to make more mistakes! Laugh at perfection!

Your mistakes are treasures, and so are you!

SHARING OUR CREATIVITY

Creativity thrives in solitude—not isolation. As creative women, we need a community.

A creative community stands strong

Julia Cameron has done this so beautifully with her life and works: The Artist's Way and Vein of Gold. All the women doing their "Morning Pages" form a telepathic creative community. Groups have formed that are inspired by these books. Whatever gets us moving, talking, collaborating creatively is a blessing.

So often, creative acts occur alone, and are shared with a few close friends or loved ones, or not shared at all.

We think we are alone

During my 12 years as a "starving artist" I doubted if I would ever be read or acknowledged creatively. Whatever I sent out was rejected, whatever I chanced to share was often misunderstood or judged harshly.

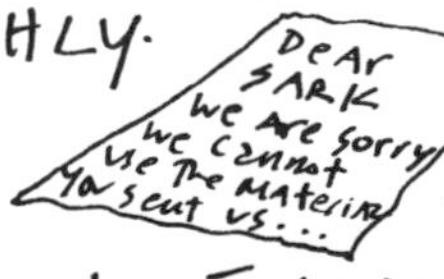
Dear SARK
We are sorry
we cannot
use the material
you sent us...

It was very lonely. I might have grown deeper roots if I'd had a community. I might have been braver about submissions, shows, or collaboration opportunities.

So I created a "community" out of my friends and

loved ones, and relied heavily on their support, insight, and encouragement.

We grow in the company of others

Like plants or flowers

Still I longed for a wider community. I dreamed of living with other creative souls, trading art supplies and inspirations.

Somehow I kept creating. I widened my community by reading and dreaming and using the

The phone connects us all

If we can connect in groups, by phone or e mail, at bookstores, churches, and teahouses, if we can share our creative spirit with other women, we will bloom and ripen and grow.

Find just one friend who likes this idea. Form a creative duo. Check in with each other and start making gentle plans—you can share art supplies!

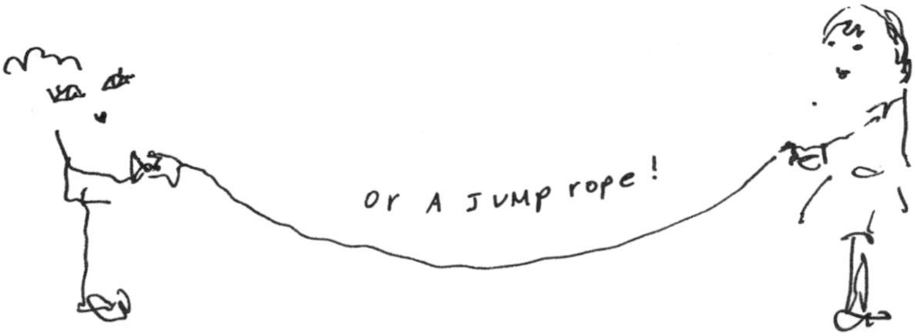
or a jump rope!

Creative expression

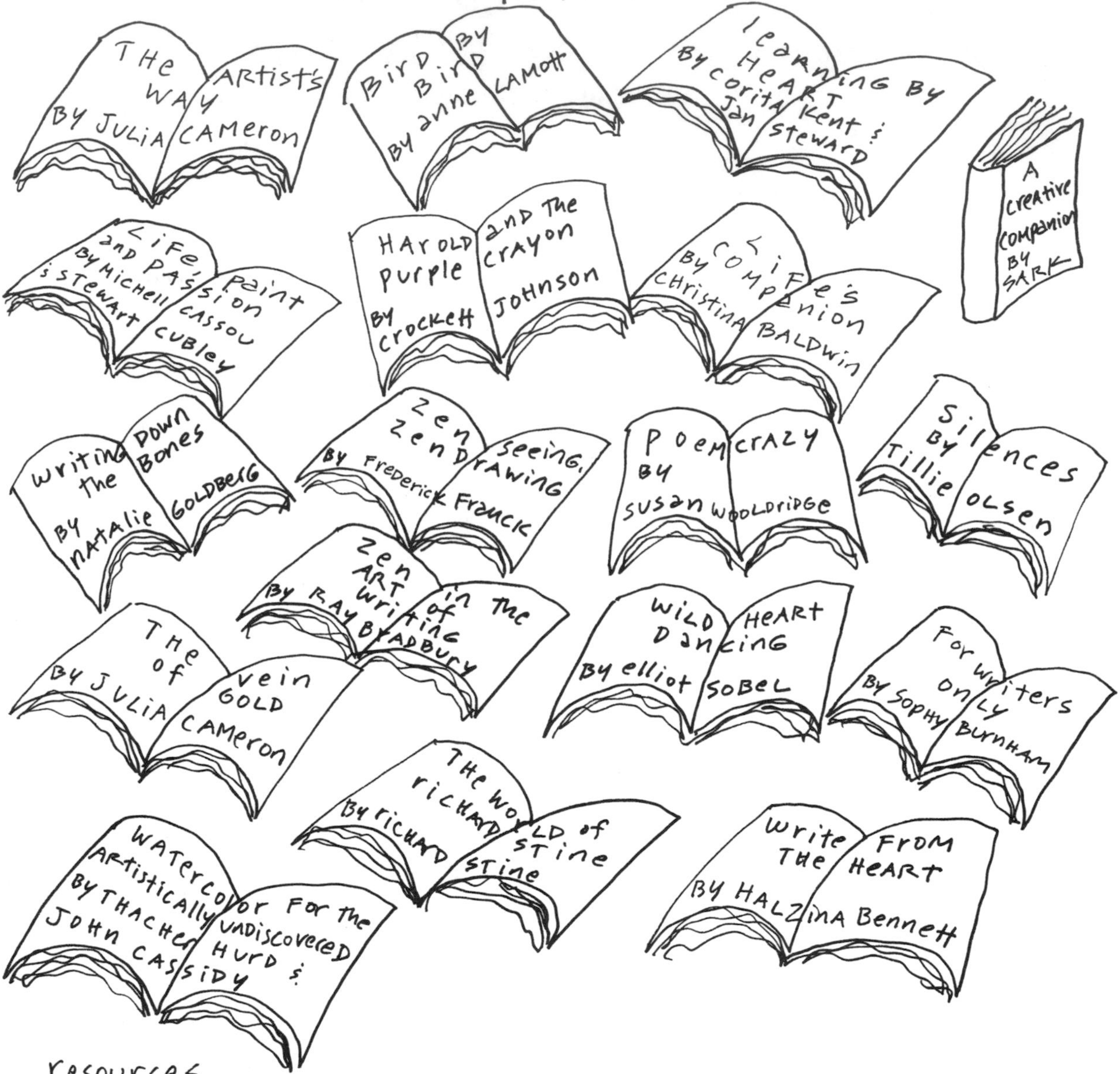
The Artist's Way By Julia Cameron
Bird by Bird By anne Lamott
learning by Heart By Corita Kent & Jan Steward
A Creative Companion By SARK
Life, Paint and Passion By Michell Cassou & Stewart Cubley
Harold and the Purple Crayon By Crockett Johnson
Life's Companion By Christina Baldwin
Writing Down the Bones By Natalie Goldberg
Zen Seeing, Zen Drawing By Frederick Franck
Poemcrazy By Susan Wooldridge
Silences By Tillie Olsen
Zen in the Art of Writing By Ray Bradbury
The Vein of Gold By Julia Cameron
Wild Heart Dancing By elliot Sobel
For Writers Only By Sophy Burnham
The World of Richard Stine By Richard Stine
Watercolor for the Artistically Undiscovered By Thacher Hurd & John Cassidy
Write From the Heart By Hal Zina Bennett

resources

- The Sun – A Magazine of ideas, a lively literary magazine of ideas and intelligent words – 1 year $32. Write P.O. Box 3000, Denville NJ 07834 or call 800·875·2997
- intuition Magazine for the Higher potential of the Mind 6 issues for $19.95 · PO Box 460773 · SF CA 94146 or call 415·949·4240

Music

- Tea for the Tillerman by Cat Stevens
- Tapestry by Carole King

How to explore money

"Relax. Your money is not your life! It just feels that way sometimes." SARK, (from the poster, "How to relax about money").

Women are exploring money in their lives now more than ever before. Money is beginning to flow into more women's lives as we become more visible, more "of the world."

Money
is
Beginning
To
Flow

Women have had a long history of money scarcity and the shifting of this is profound. Most new small businesses today are owned by women.

Money can be such a mystery. We need to be able to study its energy, accept abundance, and also learn about the gifts of not having money.

The dance of money can feel all-encompassing, energizing or draining, a curse or a lesson.

Dance of Money

Often, women are dependent financially, and afraid to upset any money balance they may have achieved.

I believe that women deserve to be financially compensated for child care and household management—if that is their life situation.

I grew up with a mother who was raised with money, and a father who was not. This created interesting money issues for me. I'm either generous or frugal, and have a lot to learn about the "middle."

Women are frequently in a fog about money—the finite and detailed issues of investing, savings, tax planning, and estate management are something

"For later," "For someone else to do."

The more responsibility women take for their financial lives, the more money will be available to them.

As my business has expanded, and more books have sold, my income has also grown. This has brought new challenges of distribution, planning, investing, and other matters I've never faced. I keep thinking that I shouldn't have to do it all alone. Yet of course I don't, because I have a staff and there are professionals to help. It reminds me of my blocks about math—that girls weren't good at it—so I wasn't.

I let my blocks about math wall me in . . .

Women are just as smart about money as any man, and just as deserving to have a lot of it.

Women can:

- study money
- make friends with money
- channel money to others
- accept money
- step into financial power
- open up new money makers

Your talents and energies deserve financial reward! Women can open up more to the subject of deserving. We think it's selfish to want too much. We minimize our needs and stifle our own growth.

"Well, I don't need much."

The world hears that and responds accordingly.

STUDY MONEY: Open up the subject in your life. Read books about money. Have conversations with other people. Keep a money journal about your patterns and habits, successes and weaknesses.

My Money Life

MAKE FRIENDS WITH MONEY: Find joy-full ways to play with money. Stop speaking negatively about it. Encourage gratefulness for whatever you have.

MAGNIFY POSITIVE MONEY FEELINGS.

I AM WEALTHY on the inside

CHANNEL MONEY TO OTHERS: Practice tithing—a percentage of your income to whatever you feel is good or nourishing for others.

GIVE MONEY AWAY WITH NO STRINGS ATTACHED. (It can be a tiny amount). Give money anonymously or secretly (the energy increases without your ego involved).

ACCEPT MONEY: Stop fighting for the meal check! Allow others to "gift" you. Accept presents graciously and gratefully.

OPEN UP NEW MONEY MAKERS: Create income "streams"

income streams

that can flow without your direct involvement. This can be in the form of dividends, royalties, or commissions.

These income streams can expand with time to fund other plans you may have.

Money is fascinating, fun, mysterious, and invigorating.

<u>You can create money</u>

- WHAT Are your Financial Dreams?
- How Does Money scare you?
- How Does Money save you?
- WHAT can you learn About Money?

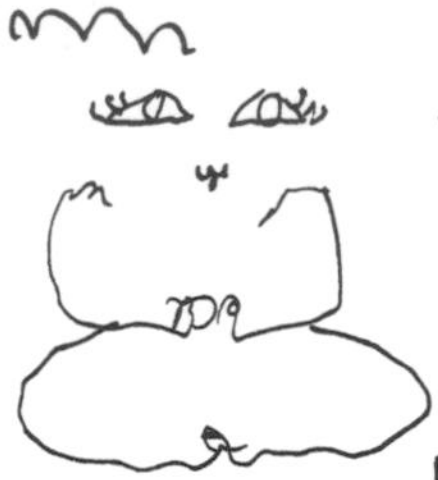

Sit with your Money Feelings

We Are not taught enough Money lessons—especially not About creating Money in Healthy, innovative ways. We need to Be our own teachers and call upon others for Help.

I was in A Money Group with some women that felt so power·full it scared us and we quit.

It is now O.K. to Be Financially successful.

I Have realized that my own needs Are fairly simple, But my vision for the world is Huge and costly.

I envision: (Among other things)

- an Artist's and writer's Bank.
- The SARK Foundation: providing creative support to Artists, children and old people.
- Brand new plan for Arts in All schools.
- the unions of nursing Homes, child care, and Humane societies.
- prosperous libraries.

WHAT else? WHAT Are your Glorious visions for the world?

We can Build and create miracles

We can create Money

How to Form a Money Group

Money

- Find several women who are interested and open to exploring money in their lives.

- Meet monthly or weekly if motivated.
- Choose a book to work with (see resources).
- Make a time commitment 1-3-6-12 months or weeks (exploring money will bring up lots of feelings and it may be tempting to quit. Providing some structure will help).
- Choose a facilitator, or rotate each time. One person needs to be responsible to the "assignment" chosen and manage the time so that the group doesn't dissipate its energy "chatting."
- Keep notes: your money group is revolutionary and deserves recording. You may want to help other women form money groups.

MONEY

let money be a flying carpet in your life
use it to travel to where you want to go

How to Accept power

You Are A power-Full Woman

How Does this Feel? Do you embrace it or push it aside? The subject of power isn't explored very much or taught in schools, or even by parents. Luckily, this is beginning to change.

People see me as a power-Full woman. Yet, I don't see it myself. Why?

We are endowed with power by our very birth, and then shrouded from the knowledge and acceptance of it. My Mother is a power-Full woman. When I comment on it, she laughs and says, "Oh no, I'm not."

WHAT Do we think power is?

Power: A
Spirit or
Divinity...

The Dictionary says:

"Ability to do, act, or produce," "Great ability to do, act or affect strongly; vigor; force; strength," "A spirit or divinity."

I think we must study power and what it means to us as women. power means to me:

- Standing strongly in your own center and living from your heart.
- Truth-telling, wisdom, and strength. How often do we think of power?

Think of your women friends.

Identify the ones you consider power-Full. Why? What qualities do they share?

How can we increase healthy power as women?

Consider:

- spiritual power
- physical power
- financial power
- emotional power
- psychic power
- healing power
- love power

POWER

In what ways are you power-full? In what ways do you feel less power-full? Do you think of power consciously?

When I think of power-full female role models, I think of:

Athena, Amelia Earhart, Maya Angelou, Sylvia Beach, Mother Teresa, All Mothers, Eleanor Roosevelt, Oprah Winfrey, Elisabeth Kübler-Ross, Bette Midler, Barbra Streisand (there are so many fantastic and power-full women!)

In what ways are you like these women? Different?

We need new definitions of power. It is not "power over" I'm interested in. I think that as women, we think that it isn't nice to talk about power. Or, we think of power as domination. Power needs to be re-visioned for women.

It's time for us to create power, be visible power-fully, and accept power.

I envision a world full of power-full women, who know it and act from it. Imagine the miracles we can create!

Living with Money, Living without Money

My grandfather was an entrepreneur who created his own income, my father worked for a corporation for 39 years. The differences were striking to me. My father spent 6 days a week traveling during much of my early childhood. I wish he could have owned his own business and been home.

After my 250 jobs, trying to get money illegally, studying millionaires, and living without money for 12 years, I decided to try and live with money.

In 1989, I invented something called "spiritcards," which were handmade art piece affirmations. I created a display for them, and put them in a store. That led to hand made affirmation books, and then inspirational posters.

I made 12,000 posters by hand in my garage, using spray mount, colored pens, and color xerox.

The posters were sold in a catalog and the first one, "How to Be an Artist," led me to write a whole series of 17 more.

How to Be an Artist
How to Be really Alive
How to really love A child
Cats Are angels with Fur
Dogs Are Miracles with Paws
How to relax About Money
In-spiration Guide
Being A wonder Ful Friend
invite someone Dangerous to tea

Then my books were published. visions of posters danced in my head

I then hired a business mentor to work with me on a daily basis so I could learn about business and create a company that would support my visions and creativity.

Camp SARK was born in 1993, and now has a staff of 3, consultants, interns, a subscription "Museletter," a licensing division, and plans for the SARK Foundation.

 I planted an impossible garden, and it's blooming ecstatically

I AM an Author and Artist who is Living My Dream, and owns A company. (the kind of company I Always wanted to work for).

I stay at home and work in pajamas. I still procrastinate and get scared.

Here are *some* things I've learned About Living with Money: I'm still learning!

- Money Doesn't solve All problems. It makes some things easier, and some more difficult.
- When you have money, others may want some. then you must decide.
- Living with money responsibly must be studied.
- Money can act as an insulator and separate you from others.
- People can get jealous and judgmental about your money and how you choose to spend it.
- Living with money can cause fears of living without money to resurface.
- Hoarding, cheapness, extravagance, poor planning can all sabotage.
- Money guilt can occur.
- You might have money, and your friends might not. How is that?
- Sharing money is more complicated than it seems.
- Money is really fun and can provide outstanding environments. What happens in those environments is still up to you.

I'm in my pajamas more than I'm out of them

Fun Money

My parents were always worried about my not having money during my years as a starving artist. Then, when I got some money, they worried about what I was going to do with the money!

Here are some specific ways I lived without money, and my recommendations for those who wish to try:

The dinner tree had plates in the branches

- Start a "Dinner tree" where you ask a different friend each night to share their dinner with you. 7 friends = 7 nights.
- Develop an appetite for simple foods.
- Think of ways to trade for rent: childcare, eldercare, housesitting.
- Use the library a lot, books will nourish you.

A good thick book filled her up

- Spend lots of time walking outside – it will physically refresh you.
- Devote yourself to some art – you won't notice poverty as much.
- Refuse to be shamed by poverty or be judged by society as inferior.
- Ask for help. Develop your humility.

Stand on top of a tall hill
fling your arms wide
and shout,

"O.K. I owe everyone!!!"

- risk owing people.
- realize that you can choose to create money.
- study money as an energy.

Creating Money
by
Sanaya Roman
Duane Packer

- realize that many of the great artists, poets, and spiritual teachers were poor.
- Live your dream and realize that the money is important, but incidental.
- invest in your **self** your dreams, talents, and abilities.

YOU ARE WORTHY OF INVESTMENT

- Live as powerfully as you are able without money— develop your spiritual gifts.
- read about people who didn't have money: <u>A Tree Grows in Brooklyn</u> by Betty Smith, <u>Hunger</u> by Knut Hamsun, anything by Henry Miller.
- concentrate on learning to love your self.

MAY YOUR MONEY CHOICES COME FROM YOUR HEART.

Money and power

Creating Money
By Sanaya Roman & Duane Packer
Transforming your Dragons
By Jose Stevens Ph.D.
Six Months off
By Hope Dlugozima, James Scott & David Sharp
Visionary Business
By Marc Allen
To Build the Life you want, create the work you love
By Marsha Sinetar
Your Money or your Life
By Joe Dominguez and Vicki Robin
I Could Do anything if only I knew what it was
By Barbara Sher
You'll see it when you believe it
By Dr. Wayne Dyer
Do What you Love The Money will Follow
By Marsha Sinetar
Money Meditations for Women
By Jo Ann Lordahl
Seven Laws of Money
By Michael Phillips
Creative Visualization
Creative Visualization
By Shakti Gawain
Max Makes a Million
By Maira Kalman

resources

- an income of Her own – For teens Ages 13–19 who want to know what it takes to form their own Businesses. For information: 804 W. Burbank Blvd., Burbank, CA 91506 or call 818·842·3040
- Women incorporated – Nationwide support for women in Business with access to capital, discounts on office supplies, shipping, accounting services and Health insurance. $29 for one year – newsletter: 1401 21st St., Ste. 310, Sacramento, CA 95814. or call 800·930·3993.

Music

- Pachelbel Canon by Gordon Jeffries
- Tongues by Gabrielle Roth and the Mirrors

Isabel

I first saw her in Big Sur, in the patio of a cliffside restaurant. She was sailing through, wearing wildly painted leather shoes, a very bright white blouse, and her white hair swept elegantly on top of her head.

I said to myself, "there's my new friend!" Then, I was struck by shyness and couldn't get up to meet her. An hour later, I saw her in the parking lot, getting into a big car with her women friends. I knew then that I had to meet her— and rushed over to give her a copy of my poster "How to be an Artist."

She beamed at me, stopped and read the poster out loud, in its entirety, in her New Zealand accent.

She then said,

"Why don't you give me a call in Berkeley, dear!"

When I first visited her, she flung the door open, looked intently at me and said,

"My dear. Come in and lie down immediately! You look very nappish."

She brought me out to her marvelous garden, and I laid down on a brightly colored mat in the sun.

She then brought me succulent bits of food on tiny plates. I said to her,

"Isabel, may I ask you a personal question?"

"Well yes, I hope it is personal!"

"Were you ever married?"

She replied impishly, "No, I escaped that particular thing."

Isabel owned a sportswear design company and had her own factory for 22 years. She traveled in "high society" and had famous mentors. Yet, she doesn't speak of herself very much or often—you must be patient to find things out about her. She is consistently curious about other people and their stories.

Her home reflects her taste and style and is filled with flowers, bright colors, fabulous artwork, and simplicity.

Isabel is one of the wisest souls and youngest spirits I know. Once on a trip together, I found her on the balcony outside our room, with a flower in her hand, peering intently down. I asked her what she was doing.

"I'm looking into the hearts of flowers with this magnifying glass. Come see!"

A whole world is inside the heart of a flower

Her approach to life is one of "fresh mind" and alive choices. Isabel gulps life.

She is also rather mysterious and quite reserved. She says she was raised by the "last of the Victorians."

Isabel can so graciously decline an invitation, you don't even realize for awhile that she's said no!

One time, I rented a house on top of a mountain in Big Sur for my 39th birthday, and invited Isabel for brunch. During the night, the rains had washed the roads out, and people coming to the party were digging their cars out of muddy ditches by the side of the road. People were also calling to say that they wouldn't be coming due to the weather. All of a sudden, there was Isabel, who had driven her 1968 Plymouth Fury right up that washed out mountain road! She swept in with a big smile and basket of fresh muffins.

To Isabel, everything is brand new and the world is a wonder.

Once my friend Brigette was in a car with Isabel and suddenly Isabel called out, "Oh look! Succulents!" Brigette thought she was talking about succulence, but Isabel had leapt out of the car to greet the succulent green plants she had spotted from the car window.

Isabel most definitely lives juicy!

"Not for me the pale shades of anonymity, but the hot lush colors of imagination, creativity, and accomplishment." Isabel

Adrienne

She came to interview me for a column she wrote, and as soon as I saw her, I yelled out, "Oh! I just love you already!"

Her face and essence had completely captivated me. When I first heard her laugh, I knew we'd be friends forever.

Adrienne is beautiful, funny, irreverent, talented, sexy, and quite outrageous. She is also driven, highly sensitive, relentless, and a perfectionist (Did I say stubborn?)

She sat in the Magic Cottage in my hanging chair and said I should meet her boyfriend. I thought, "Oh no. He won't be her equal, and I probably won't like him."

The moment I met Ken, I felt a rush of love that continues to this day. (And he is very much her equal!)

Adrienne's love relationship was a model of the kind of relationship I wanted one day—romantic, honest, deeply loving with lots of play and humor. I read poetry at their wedding.

I watch closely as Adrienne practices "intimate negotiations" and transparent sharing of feelings. I marvel at her ability to share her feelings—they just float out—raw, sometimes edgy, and in the moment.

She doesn't question our friendship and its strength to hold feelings. This gives me strength.

When I met her family, I named them "Functional Family Camp." At dinner, her father asked everyone to join hands and speak about how they were feeling!

Later I said to Adrienne in a jealous moment, "you're so lucky. your parents are so great!"

Her eyes darted,

"They weren't always this way!"

They had been in therapy and worked on, and are working on, their issues.

Then Adrienne and Ken had a baby named Zoe and asked me to be godmother. They are an adopted family for me.

I've learned so much soaking in the very real glow of Adrienne. Her realness and flaws inspire me to share mine (she's saying "What flaws!?").

I wish everyone could know Adrienne, which is one of the reasons I'm writing about her here. Her spirit is very bright and will and does travel far. She is a writer and has much to say—motherhood, intimate partnership, friendship.

She is also the creative director of our company, Camp SARK, and we've created SARK's Magic Museletter (she would want me to say that you can subscribe. HA!).

The succulence of Adrienne is profound and affects my life everyday.

The Life of Adrienne is an
open Book of Love

Giselle

She has wild unruly red hair that sticks out everywhere and she doesn't hide her crabbiness. Giselle reminds me of Pippi Longstocking— All grown up. (remember Pippi? Great children's book character).

Giselle is an olympic weight lifter. One of her American records is for the SNATCH, which she will tell you with a devilish grin.

She also designs amazing clothing and scarves, which are sold all over the world. Her loft space is filled with looms and beautiful women helpers with names like Venus.

Just hearing about her schedule exhausts me, yet I've enjoyed a time with her and her endearing husband Earl, sprawled on pillows in front of their fireplace. We roasted marshmallows, and talked about everything and nothing (she likes them lightly toasted).

She has the ability to work deep, and relax deep. It's a good combination.

Giselle is very literal. When I called to tell her that I was putting her in my book, she thought I meant address book! Being around Giselle is a refreshing experience. There is very little chatting or small talk.

Giselle is one of the most direct, sometimes abrupt, women I've ever met. It shocks me. One time I said,

"I've missed you," and she replied,

"Why? We hardly ever see each other."

Her tone was calm and simple and makes me realize that many people don't just "say it straight."

I explained my theory of being telepathic friends to Giselle—where you speak on the phone or just telepathically, without making plans—I don't think it's a familiar way to her, as her way isn't to me. Yet her directness is invigorating to me and you can tell where you stand.

Giselle is quick, penetrating, funny, eccentric, endearing, and very wild in spirit. She is open, animated, and deep.

She is also prone to outbursts and sudden angers that can seem alarming, until you know her heart is good. Just knowing Giselle is definitely a wild succulent experience! (and her mother Harriet is awesome).

Giselle is a woman who inspires courage and physical action. I am so glad to have a character like her in the world.

Marjorie Elaine Anderson Kennedy

My Mother is a succulent wild woman. She is the "SARK" among her friends.

She was in the Marines, and was the first female cigarette representative in the Midwest. In her 20's, she lived in a boarding house in San Francisco, and demonstrated steam irons in the window of a hardware store. She used to walk near the cottage I live in now, over 50 years ago, and dream of living in San Francisco!

A sore wisdom tooth led her back to Minnesota, where she met and married my father, Art.

Her commitment to family gave me a lot. She was there everyday and managed the kids and house with a small income and no car, while her husband traveled most of each week as a salesman.

She was imperfect and made mistakes. She also initiated going to family therapy in the early 1960's. She talked fairly openly about our family problems when most of her friends didn't.

I've often thought that if we'd had a really good family therapist, we could have resolved, or at least uncovered, the sibling incest and other problems that were so devastating to our family.

Still, there was love, and I named my Mother

"Marvelous Marge" and now her mail comes addressed to her that way!

Dear Marvelous,

Sometimes when she isn't so marvelous we call her "Marge the Sarge."

My mother can be intimidating and intense. She is also prickly, controlling, and extremely opinionated (it's scary to write about my mother's flaws).

When I called to ask her if I could include this portrait, and confessed to being nervous about her reading this book, she said,

"Susan. I told you a long time ago. You write what you need to, for you. Not for me or what I think, or what anyone else thinks!"

After soaking in these words, I said,

"Thank you. I also need to confess that I've been the recipient of you having strong feelings about things I've written, which you hoard and then attack me later with!"

She laughed. "Yes. I suppose I do do that. But you're just going to have to learn to ignore it!"

And so, I shall.

When I asked my mother what she is most grateful for, she replied,

"elastic!"

My mother also knows how to, and has, hypnotized chickens.

Women's Friendships

Some of my greatest, deepest, most gloriously intimate friendships have been and are, with women.

I have also felt horrified, afraid of exploring the dark side, and unable to practice fair fighting—or any fighting—with my women friends.

There is such rich terrain to explore in women's friendships. All or most of us have mothers, and often we project our unresolved mother issues onto our women friends.

My particular method was to: leave when it got ugly. Sometimes this is good. Sometimes there was more to uncover that could have created a better resolution and ending. "Nice girls" don't fight. Yet not fighting ended almost every friendship I had that developed problems.

One or both of us was so afraid to go into the darkness together, to speak our truths and to describe our experience.

These truths would have been oxygen—some of my friendships ended by suffocation.

I tried to pretend everything was "just fine"

I would be so afraid of losing a friend that I didn't tell the truth, and would lose her anyway.

We strike unconscious bargains with our women friends. One of mine was: I won't tell the truth if you won't leave me. This worked well as a vicious cycle.

vicious cycle

I've learned very piercingly how the unspoken can deprive a friendship of real nourishment. The timing of that speaking is crucial.

Telling a friend you don't like her boyfriend early in their relationship, or later if she hasn't asked you, can be lethal.

Repressing anger is common among women. We fear the outcome if we express it—yet repressed anger turns poisonous and ends friendships. let your anger out in responsible and conscious ways... eventually, let it go...

My friendship history and style has taught me a great deal, and the lessons I've learned help me in my current friendships.

My first friend was named Missy. She lived next door when I was very young and had lots of sisters and one brother. This was a fantastic world to me—all these siblings—I only had one brother. I remember moving away from the neighborhood when I was 11, and thinking I would die without Missy. i didn't die, but i sure missed Missy!

My next important friend was in high school. Leigh challenged me, woke me up early and invited me out to play in the world. Thank you Leigh!

My college roommate is still a very dear friend. Sally was the most grounded friend I'd ever had, and we also hitch hiked all over Tampa together, causing commotion during college.

After college, there was Julie. We were "Best Friends" for many years, and in some ways, that friendship helped me to truly grow up. Bless you Julie

When I moved to San Francisco, I had a ten-year friendship with Helen. Helen was my first real adult friend. I wish we'd learned to fight and resolve conflict—perhaps our friendship could have continued.

My women friends now—Adrienne, Susan B., Brigette, Nancy, Robin, Tori, Joe, Eleanor, Diana, Elizabeth K, Vanessa, Isabel, Elissa, Vimala, Angela, Cecilia, Debbie E, Susan H., Kathryn, Katie, Nicole, and Debra are all contributors to my health and sanity and support me by telling and hearing the truth. I love them each dearly.

These circles of
women are power-full

I believe that these circles of women around us weave invisible nets of love that carry us when we're weak and sing with us when we're strong. Let's lean back and let the arms of women's friendships carry us and help us to know ourselves better, and live our lives together.

- Who are your real friends?
- Do their faces light up when they see you?
- Are they able to celebrate your successes?
- Do you tell each other the truth?
- Do you have ways to resolve conflicts?
- Do you need more friends?

How do women's friendships nourish and support you?

Are you a marvelous friend?

How to Make Friends
(at any age)

Go out: This sounds obvious, but sometimes we forget that in our homes, the chances of making new friends is rather slim. Although, you could try neighbors, mailpersons, children you could invite them in— "import-a-friend!"

Change routines: Our habits can insulate us from new people and experiences. If we go somewhere new, we might meet someone new.

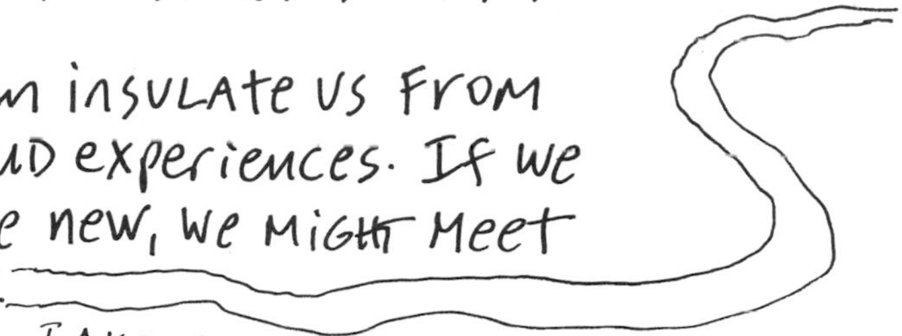

TAKE A BRAND NEW PATH

Be available for friendship: People will not know that you're interested in friendship unless you indicate it somehow. A smile, a comment, an invitation, a phone call, a note, are all good ways.

welcome
to
the
neighborhood
we love it here!

Join something: It doesn't matter what you join— you could meet someone who could be a friend.

Meditation Friends

Redefine friendship: There are so many kinds of friends. Shopping friends, carpool friends, game playing friends, phone friends, club friends, computer friends.

invent new kinds of friendships
of various ages

See where you could use some more friends, and then find some!

Change your Attitude: We all want friendship, yet we all experience friendship scarcity. Being a good friend to yourself will encourage others to want to be friends with you. Create a grateful, receptive attitude even if you don't always feel that way. It is easy to blame others for friendship failures. The failure is usually with ourselves.

Be Brave: Finding friendship can sometimes feel scary and vulnerable. We all have memories of rejection. Be your most courageous self.

Be Ageless: Consider making friends outside your own age group. Often, people of different ages can be good matches in energy and interest levels.

Be inventive: See if someone dining alone wants to eat together. (My mother recently did this with great success. She said to me, "Wasn't that a succulent wild woman thing to do?") Yes, it was! You can gently and intuitively give new people chances to include you. Try it.

Remember: Give someone the gift of being friends with YOU!

Portraits of Succulent Wild Women

At 70
By May Sarton
ain't I a Woman!
edited by Illona Linthwaite
Dance of anger
By Harriet Lerner Ph.D.
earthly Paradise
By Colette
embracing our essence
By Susan Skog
The Diary of Anaïs Nin
edited with an introduction by Gunther Stuhlmann
Goddesses in everywoman
By Jean Shinoda Bolen, M.D.
Jenny Read
By Jenny Read
Antioch University w Colo Press
1982 Burnsville, NC
The Seasons of Women
edited by Gloria Norris
Women Who Dare
By Katherine Martin
I Shock Myself
By Beatrice Wood
The Heart of a Woman
By Maya Angelou
Girl Friends
By Carmen Renee Berry and Tamara Traeder
The Girlfriends Keepsake Book
By Carmen Renee Berry and Tamara Traeder
Lip Service: The truth About Women's Darker Side in Love, Sex and Friendship
By Kate Fillion
Elsa I Come with My Songs
By Elsa Gidlow
The New Older Woman
By Peggy Downes, Ilene Tuttle, Patricia Faul & Virginia Mudd
Women Make the Best Friends
By Lois Wyse

MUSIC

- Coming Around Again by Carly Simon
- In My tribe by 10,000 Maniacs
- Amtrak Blues by Alberta Hunter

Succulent Wild Woman Groups

Groups are a great way to "Dance with your Wonder-Full self" in the company of others! They can be very spontaneous and informal, or more organized.

Here are some types of "Groups"

- Phone Group: I have entire friendships that take place on voicemail. My friend Susan and I leave 5-6 messages at a time for each other that are like little radio programs. We save them and listen with a cup of tea when the mood is right. You can also provide support and encouragement on the phone by reading quotes or poems, remembering special dates, or making "support calls" to each other.

A friendship that dances telepathically on the phone lines

- Activity Group: Succulent Wild Women are excellent company. Having tea parties, going out to wild dance clubs, reading succulent books, moonlight hiking, and grown-up slumber parties are some ways to expand your pleasure options. It's like having a bank of people you can draw interest on.

- Food Group: Succulent Wild Women love to eat! and could share favorite restaurants, delicious food, and fascinating conversations. Women can be such nourishment for each other.

They sat at separate tables and had inspiring conversation

MAKE and design new money with women and color on it!

- Money Group: Succulent Wild Women are rich and can share their knowledge of inner and outer wealth. You can practice techniques to draw money to you, or to learn how and where to share it and to make money safe, fun, and relaxing!

100 ways to feel joy

- Creativity Group: Succulent Wild Women are curious and have creative appetites. Meet at midnight, full moon, with journals and sleeping bags. Gather in drumming circles, painting classes, or sculpture gardens. Bring sketchbooks to a playground. Hire male models to pose in a drawing salon at your home.

Full moon drumming journal play

Invent your own group and format. Here is a list I use for SARK gatherings of Succulent Wild Women:

the remarkable Susan

1. Everyone is a star (making and naming stars)
2. Circles of ecstasy (stories of ecstatic moments)
3. Journey into the darkness (journal and art to find treasures of the dark)
4. Radical self-acceptance (how to experience more)
5. Fresh love (giving it to ourselves/others)
6. Wild imaginings (journaling/sharing entries)
7. "I want" exercise (writing/art to list wants)

8. creative validation (what is it? how to give/receive it)

9. splendidly imperfect (lists, admissions, acceptance)

10. micromovement support (how to begin/continue)
tiny little steps

11. eating mangoes naked (and other succulent acts)

12. invite someone dangerous to tea (wild tea parties)

Their tea cups floated above the table and steam developed faces

If you would like to receive a free expanded guideline of this material in order to begin or lead your own "Succulent Wild Woman" group, send a self-addressed stamped  envelope  to Camp SARK, P.O. Box 330039
SARKFrancisco, CA 94133
Attn: Succulent Wild Woman Groups

I'm currently recovering from a terror of groups and always avoided them. Then I joined one that is healing, fun, and very grounding.

Women meeting in groups creates an energy that is very power-full. Please explore the possibilities of more groups in your life — I send you new energy for it!

Connected and in Touch

"Stay in touch!" "Let's have lunch!" "We'll have to get together soon."

We all toss these phrases around because we genuinely want the connection, or we don't know what else to say.

Women are infused with niceness to the extent that they don't tell the truth about connection.

It was easier in kindergarten. You could just point to another girl or boy and say "Let's be friends!" and you were.

We all have different levels of energy for friendship at different times. If you don't feel an honest friendship response, set the woman free to make another friend!

Being passive-aggressive can be rampant among women. Listening to phone messages that are draining—out of obligation, promising to "have lunch soon" when you don't really want to, avoidance, "white lies," and doing activities out of fear, obligation, or guilt are all examples (Fear, Obligation, Guilt spell FOG. Don't do it!)

If we can all promote truth-telling with women seeking connection, there will be plenty for everyone!

We've all been in both positions: seeking and being sought after.

Here's a possible response to someone seeking when you would rather not continue or expand the connection.

"Thanks for asking me to ______. I need to be honest and say that my availability for friendship right now may be different from yours, but thank you for thinking of me."

If you can practice this in your own language, and until you feel comfortable saying it, you will add so much to the integrity of your connections.

I used to feel that I had to connect somehow with everyone who asked. I now see that it was related to my lack of boundaries, desire to merge, and fear of judgment. (of course sometimes, I just didn't like the person!)

Now I remember this when I am seeking connection, and if it somehow isn't working out with the other person, I try not to take it personally. I invest in a source that's more ripe.

note: sometimes I fail in this attempt and feel rejected!

Serendipity is a good indicator. When serendipity is at play, there is an effortless quality to connecting. When the connecting is an effort or struggle, sometimes it is a sign to let go, or at least loosen up.

Check with your body. It knows almost instantly if the connection is a good one.

There are so many excellent women to know! Find the nourishing, inspiring, endearing women. Hold them close. Cup their little faces in your hands and say "You are good and adorable! I like you so much!"

WAYS TO SHARE SUCCULENCE

WOMEN SHARING SUCCULENCE IS A JOY!

We are all givers, and can also allow our receiving abilities to grow wilder.

SHARING SUCCULENCE CAN BE:

- Getting a white cotton shirt and writing a tribute to your friend on it.
- Dedicating your phone message to a friend for a day—or a week.
- Making or sending an anonymous book of poetry.
- Assembling a book or collage of her amazing qualities.
- Setting up a "Mystery date or trip" for you and a friend.
- Offering to wash her hair.
- Sharing clothes you don't normally wear.
- Letting a friend read your journal.
- Going on a "miracle walk" and hiding treasures along the way for your friend to find.
- Meeting for a picnic and having surprise friends there.

RECEIVING SUCCULENCE CAN BE:

- Asking for keen listening—no solutions.
- Allowing a friend to clean your scary drain. (thank you Brigette and Susan!)
- Opening a book to your favorite part and letting yourself be read to.
- Daring to say "would you rub my neck?" no reciprocation.
- Making a list of ways you enjoy receiving.
- Making a list of ways you block receiving.

Let your giving inspire your receiving. Realize that we cannot truly give without receiving.

WHAT is succulent in your life that you want more of?

Ask 3 friends to call you 3 times during the day and leave you messages of things they like about you.

I called all my mother's friends and said "lets not wait until my mom dies to say what we so loved about her—would you please tell me now?" I then made a book of what they said. She treasures this book.

We need to express our most succulent selves—sooner, deeper, and more often!

Mentoring

Our treasures must be shared. Mentoring is a way of creating a laboratory or a tiny community in which succulence can grow. it can grow into a magnificent flower

Do you remember informal mentors early in life? One of mine was Cecilia. She was old and lived alone, and seemed to love it. I went to her house and presented theatrical monologues that I would write and perform. I remember her acceptance of my essence and how safe I felt there.

I also remember plate-sized chocolate chip cookies and trays of African violets on the windowsills

One of my writing mentors was my 5th grade teacher who loved what I wrote and encouraged me to write more.

My 1st grade teacher, Mrs. Gooler, was my library and reading mentor. She inspired me to get a library card and read a book a day. She would also send me to the 5th grade class to read out loud to them.

The Wonderful Flight to the Mushroom Planet
Cricket in Times Square

visions of books danced in my head

My grandfather was my traveling mentor. He encouraged me to keep a journal on trips and then read my writings to him when I got back.

Miriam was my art/life mentor. She bought my original artwork at inflated prices and advised me on my "pattern of living."

Now in my 40's, I am a mentor for others—through my books, and more personally with younger friends.

Mentoring is a superb way for women to share energy and gifts, to teach rituals and traditions, and to assist others in living more succulent lives.

"WHAT is A weed? A plant whose virtues HAVE never Been Discovered."

emerson

All women can Mentor, if they wish. We All HAVE specific talents, wisdom, and knowledge to share. we Forget that we can so strongly Affect others, JUST in Being who we Already Are.

Mentoring creates opportunities to continue succulent circles of women. especially if we choose not to parent, it's A way to let our Gifts continue on.

Meditate on Mentoring. See if you Feel inspired to Take Action, or Just Give others the opportunity to learn From you.

I've Been in A reciprocal Mentoring relationship with Vanessa since she was 11. She is now 17. I Definitely learn As Much From Her As she Might From Me.

(it's very inspiring For Me to realize that I was not this evolved At 17) A Good sign For the Future!

Vanessa is A Marvelous combination of electricity, Genius, and splendid imperfections. She lets me read Her Journals sometimes, and I Feel Blessed to Be Able to see WHAT Grows inside of Her.

She is the Best preview I know of For an upcoming Succulent Wild Woman. May All of our young women stand so strong, Brilliant, and Beautiful.

Growing As Wild Women

We must insist on succulence! Our lives are too rich and rare to have less. We will grow more as we practice.

Growing can be uncomfortable, loud, unfamiliar, and feel perilous to our underdeveloped personality selves.

Growing as wild women involves breaking out of cages, boxes, stereotypes, categories, and captivity. It involves standing tall, laughing loudly, and being who we really are.

"I've always wanted to cultivate modesty
but I've been far too busy."

Dame Edith Sitwell

Growing means separation from: being victims, passive-aggressive participants, unwilling caretakers, lying lovers, fake friends, or "nice girls."

Growth means change: change your attitudes, perspectives, patterns, and habits.

Succulent wild women are inside all of us. We can invite them out to play!

Growing means letting go of: what others will think, of narrow possibilities, of tight clothes and uncomfortable shoes. Growing means: accepting power, telling the truth, creating miracles, and making the most alive choices.

Yes

Succulent wild women are all around you. look for the bright eyes, ready smile, and unusual clothes. Or perhaps it's a more shy succulent wild woman who dresses and appears more quiet, and then you get close enough to bask in her succulent glow.

There are so many fabulous Wild Women! Here are a few of my favorites— famous and more obscure. Please continue the list by adding your particular favorites. Our naming of these women is very important. It creates channels for others to discover them. We must remember our succulent wild women!

Dame edith Sitwell. elsa Gidlow. Beatrice Wood. Isadora Duncan. Sarah Bernhardt. ruth Gordon. Gertrude stein. Martha Graham. Miriam Wornum. Jessica Tandy. anaïs nin. Jessica Mitford. May Sarton. anne Morrow Lindbergh. Dame Sark. imogene Cunningham. Maya angelou. Madeleine L'engle. emily Dickinson. Colette.

WHO can you think of?

Draw out the wild women—in yourself and others.

We were born to be wild, I assure you.

Just look at our bodies—wild containers for our great big hearts.

I love you.

Succulent Wild Women... We Are All Connected... Circle of Women Friends... Circle of Women Friends... We Are All Connected...

For your ruminations...

- List some ways you are "Living Juicy" (words or drawings)
- new in·sights about romance (with your·self or another)
- What are you reading?
- the most alive choice you have recently made...
- Who do you admire? Why?
- Do you feel safe?
- How are you satisfied/dissatisfied?
- Succulent advice you would give younger women?
- list your most challenging, and best qualities.
- When and how are you most loving towards your·self?

Building a Succulent Community

The Womansource Catalog & Review edited by Ilene Rosoff
The Tomorrow Trap By Karen E. Peterson Ph.D
Tree Houses By Peter Nelson
Ordinary Magic By John Welwood
Mindfulness and Meaningful Work By Claude Whitmyer
Reviving Ophelia: Saving the Selves of Adolescent Girls By Mary Pipher Ph.D
Chicken Soup for the Woman's Soul By Jack Canfield, Mark Victor Hansen, Jennifer Read Hawthorne and Marci Shimoff
Where the Heart Is—A Celebration of Home edited by Julienne Bennett & Mimi Luebbermann
Tiny, Tiny Houses By Lester Walker
My Family and Other Animals By Gerald Durrell (temporarily out of print)
The Magic Cottage Address Book By SARK
How Good Do We Have to Be? By Harold Kushner

resources

The World Times (the good news newspaper) For a quarterly subscription, $29.95 (Domestic), $59.95 (international) Address: PO Box 223 N. Guadalupe, Ste. 464, Santa Fe, NM 87501, Phone: 505.424.9210

Rob Brezsny's Horoscope: 1.900.844.2500 (Approx cost is $5 per call and well worth it!)

The Letter Exchange: A place to meet other letter writers by mail. For more information, write to: PO Box 6218 Albany, CA 94706

Mentoring Hotline: learn how to become a mentor for a child. Free Brochure. 1.800.914.2212

Hope Magazine: A magazine that encourages understanding and a greater sense of possibilities; to help us glimpse the common bonds of our humanity without judgment, and to celebrate enduring human values. One year subscription 24.95, mail to Hope Magazine, PO Box 52241, Boulder, Co. 80322 or call 1.800.513.0869

Color·Full PATHWAYS

A portion of the royalties from this Book will Be Donated to charitable organizations that support women and children's rights & environmental concerns

CALL SARK's inspiration Phone Line!

415. 546. epic (3742)

For A 3-5 Minute Message recorded by SARK

A Great place to Give and receive inspiration!

24 Hours A DAY

SARK's MAGIC Museletter

A Glorious, Color·Full subscription to Fun and Adventure

Please see last page of Book For more Delicious information

TO Order SARK's First 5 BOOKS: A Creative Companion, inspiration Sandwich, SARK's Journal and play! Book, Living Juicy, The Magic Cottage Address Book

Ask your Favorite Book·store

Or Call: Celestial Arts
1. 800. 841. BOOK (2665)

or write: Po Box 7327
Berkeley CA 94707

To the WORLD of SARK

Support your
local Library
and
Favorite Book store
Thank you for reading!

Free
copies of: SARK's
Juicy Advice About
Finding a publisher and
How to form your own
Succulent Wild Woman Group
Send: A self Addressed
stamped envelope to:
CAMP SARK
Po Box 330039
SARKfrancisco CA 94133
tell us which one
you'd like! include
double postage for both!

Send SARK angel MAIL

Write to: SARK
AT CAMP SARK
po Box 330039
SF CA 94133
You'll be included on SARK's
MAGIC MAILING list!

For an updated peek into
SARK's creative schedule of
Appearances, writing sabbaticals,
and General information
About ordering SARK
Gift items, CALL
415·397·SARK (7275)
24 Hours A DAY

To order More copies of
Succulent Wild Woman, and
other Simon & Schuster titles,
CAll 1·800·223·2336
Fax 1·800·445·6991 or Send order
to: Simon & Schuster
200 OLD Tappan road
OLD Tappan New Jersey 07675
visit
Simon Says web site: HTTP//WWW.SIMONSAYS.COM
For A list of All Simon & Schuster titles look for SARK!
CAll special sales with regard to special Discounts for
Succulent Wild Woman for Groups or teachers 212·654·8552

We Are All Syncronistically Connected!

I Give BIG thanks to:

everyone who reads and shares SARK books and art
each person who calls the inspiration line
every subscriber to SARK's Magic Museletter.
All the authors, poets, film-makers and creative geniuses who inspire me!
To my dear neighbors: Sally, Michael, Richard, Curtis ♡ Nancy
To Speedys! Art, Marshall, Dorothy, Stephanie and Adam ♡
Luvy and Pat 2 walking inspirations
Special thanks to Mr. and Mrs. Jack Hammer
KKSF "Lights out San Francisco" 103.7 FM
Diane ♡ Brian houseboat love
ancient times incense
Elizabeth Kuster endearing author
Wild parrots of Telegraph Hill
isle of SARK
To my Monday night group: into. me. see.
Ray Davi the incomparable ambassador to SARK
To Nancy Cobb for truth
Family of Hildebrand ♡
Minneapolis in summer
For Tori Nethery: a wonder of a woman
Jupiter sees all
So does God
With love to my niece Emily Claire
Veronica Weaver we all love you!
For my godchild Zoe Arielle I adore you completely
Isabel Collins my "zen teacher"
To Vanessa Carlisle a growing goddess with love...
Larry Alan Rosenthal Brobdingnagian love
The Henry Miller Library an oasis of inspiration
Susan Beardsley my psychic twin
Andrew John Kennedy a hopefull and unusual historian
Giselle ♡ Earl marshmallow love
With love for Joe Brown of San Francisco
love love love infinitely
With admiration for Roy Carlisle and all at Circulus Publishing Group ♡
Adrienne ♡ Ken a true festival of loving
To Craig McNair Wilson
To: Marvelous Marjorie and in loving memory of Arthur James Kennedy and Pat Snyder Kennedy
Nicole Young, Molly, Ned, Alex an uncommon family
Diana ♡ George my fairy godparents
Carmel
"Dream Dentist" Van
To my agent and dear friend Debra Goldstein: a muse. a star. with glowing gratitude.
and to all at William Morris: I love being a client, and the percentages are fair!
Robin ♡ John indestructible love and humor
Anne Page for freedom!
To Debbie Edwards: "elegant strength"
Valerie Bleth "sister"
Eric ♡ Lesley bless your love
To Camp SARK: you are a bright and growing company I thank you
Elissa Rabellino a strong and beautiful essence
New York
To Craig D. a classy 7
To Cecilia, Lulu and Steve "cat love"
Susan ♡ Brett let's play transformation!
To Scott telepathic hands and heart
The House: love to Angela ♡ Garry Justin and Jordan Susan, Louis, Sarah, Sandy and House restaurants Go eat there!
To Brigette Scheel: camp director licensing director
a primary source of trusting life & creativity
To Adrienne Steele: creative director editor-in-chief of Magic Museletter
Feelings made safe. creative wellspring
A special note of thanks and acknowledgment to my former editor, Joann Deck. and to the publishers of my first 5 books: Celestial Arts, I am gratefull. Thank you to David Hinds and Phil Wood. ♡
Laughing periodontist "Demon Rose"
Thank you to the Camp SARK interns: Sabrina, Andrea, Lora
To my editor Mary Ann Naples: a wise, brave and remarkable woman
To Ken Davis: yes we will.
A huge round of applause & thank you to Laurie Chittenden, Jim Thiel and all at Simon & Schuster
A New York publisher with heart and courage
To Vimala Priestess of the Alphabet
To Eleanor Trausman a children's angel
Kate ♡ Max your dear souls
To Gary Rosenthal a very human therapist! with deep gratitude
San Francisco
Esalen
Sarah Lindabury Hanson for knowing me at 18 and still loving me at 42!
Katie Grant wild bright flame of talent
To Nature Stop: Edgar and John
Big Sur
Paradise Island

SARK's MAGIC Museletter

You
Are
A
Gift
To:
There is a magic cottage inside each of us

Dear Angel Faces,

I am always wanting healing to occur in a straight line, or in some kind of "connect the dots" map. Some part of me is always counting—the number of months since my father's death, the number of years since I spoke with my older brother. If only healing took place in some kind of reasonable pattern!

The seduction of a pattern is so that I can predict, rehearse, or control the outcome. I think "After more than a year since my father's death, I should be feeling ______."

I believe that healing happens in spirals and layers and inside interior crevices. It comes at 4 AM while watching the moon, or unexpectedly sobbing at a bookstore when you spot a particular book that you would have bought for your father and then you stop and suddenly remember that he is dead.

While on vacation this month, I experienced a healing realization while walking on a sandy path up from the beach. During my early childhood, my father traveled extensively on business and was gone most of each week. I have known for a long time about the loss and abandonment I experienced, but this was an intellectual knowing. I was vacationing with my dear friend Adrienne, who was spending five days away from her two-year-old daughter Zoe. I heard about how much she missed her mom, and realized that I missed my dad like this every week. Some part of me made him not real so that it wouldn't hurt so much. I see myself recreate this dynamic now with the man I love. When we're apart for a certain amount of time, I begin dismantling the relationship in some ways, and distance myself, and make him not real so that I don't experience loss.

I fell to my knees on that sandy beach path, and cried the hot tears of a young child.

Healing doesn't care about the years. I think it is ageless and timeless. It waits for our souls to shift into acceptance.

I believe we can heal ourselves, and in so doing, become "stronger at the broken places" (from Wayne Muller's book, "Legacy of the Heart").

I have so many broken places and intend to stay close to the healing spirals and mysteries of the soul.

I wish for you:

The willingness to look right at the saddest parts of yourself, and allow healing to take place

To think of yourself as "committed to healing" in your life and others' lives.

To explore healing in new, unfamiliar ways

I send to you:

A clear light shining inside of you that heals spots

A summer adventure outdoors, naked in water

A moonlight picnic

A deep humming sound from way inside you that vibrates your bones

The articulation of pain and the allowing of your healing imagination

Spontaneous prayers

To spend holy time with a child

To sit in your own essence, holding the tiny [illegible]

And a no hands bike ride!

For Love and Healing,

SARK

MAYBE

Actual size 17x24 inches

Dear Angel Faces,

Welcome to your personal invitation to the MAGIC Museletter! There is a large plant growing through the wall of my MAGIC cottage here in San Francisco. This Museletter reminds me of a magnificent, magical plant that sprouted from a dream, and is now growing into the homes of all my readers.

The Museletter was born in 1996 and now goes out to thousands of amazing people. It is the result of a wonder·full collaboration between my business partners and the entire Camp SARK clan to produce and write this for you and also features your writing, support, and feedback.

A subscription to the MAGIC Museletter enables us to mail to you huge, full-color, consistent, exciting pieces of art on a regular basis. This is so exciting to me! I myself read and get inspired by the Museletter all the time! It includes snippets of conversation, wild imaginings, and peeks into cottage life with me. I write a letter for you in each issue and I look forward to talking with you and having you along for the fun and adventure of it all!

I send you a dream cape, a hat that keeps out negativity, and goblets of inspiration.

Very Dearly,

SARK

Here's what you can look forward to in the Museletter:

- Each issue includes a 17" x 24" Inspirational letter from SARK that focuses on different themes. Some back issue themes have included: Healing, Friendship, Succulence, and Comfort
- SARK's Purple Backpack Adventures–A Traveler's Guide to Serendipity
- Inner Views–Wild Imaginings with highly creative people (which we all are!)
- Subscriber's Contribute–An opportunity for your art and writing to be published in the Museletter!
- SARK's latest calendar & book gathering dates.
- Ripe News from Camp and more!

To order back issues of the Museletter send check or money orders for $4.50 per issue (includes shipping and handling-$6.50 per issue for all foreign orders, in U.S. funds only please!) to Camp SARK, Attn: ML Back issues, PO Box 330039, SF, CA 94133.

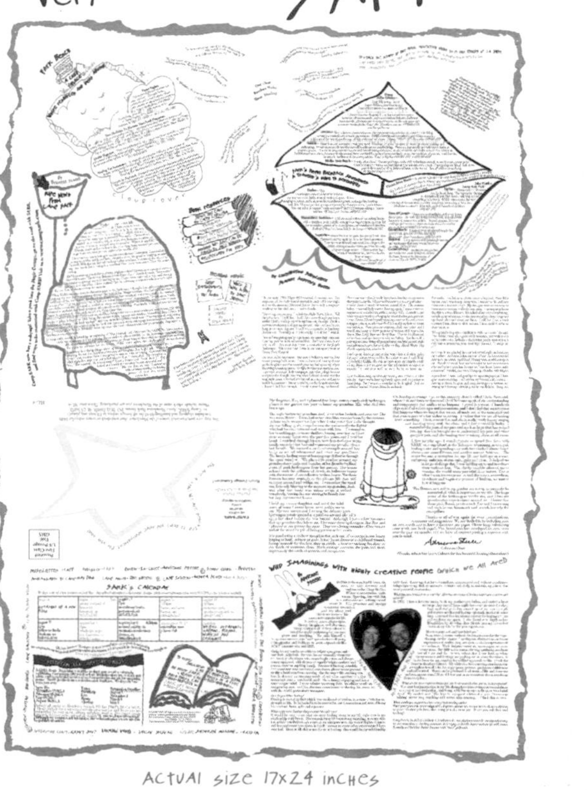

Actual size 17x24 inches

GENTLY TEAR OUT THIS PAGE AND SEND IT TO US!

YES!

Please sign me up to receive a two-year, eight-issue subscription to SARK's Magic Museletter. Please send this card (see back), along with $21 to:

Camp SARK Attn.: Museletter, PO Box 330039, SF, CA 94133.

*Checks or Money Orders Accepted. Checks made payable to Camp SARK. Regular Subscription $21, children 12 and under and "**star achieving** artists" rate $17.50. All Foreign orders $26, made payable in US funds please.*

Sign Up a Friend

There will be so much inspiration and information in **SARK's Magic Museletter,** you'll want to share it with your friends and family. The Museletter is a unique gift to give and to receive and will provide two years worth of creativity and fun at a great price! Please choose a rate for your gift subscription and send it along with your payment to the above address.

By First Class Miracles
To The Delectable
Stamp your hands clap your feet

Please allow 6-8 weeks for delivery.

FOLD HERE AND SEND TO US!

SARK's Magic Museletter

Subscriber Information

(Please print clearly!)

1

Name **Phone #** **E-mail**

Address **City** **State** **Zip (+ 4 digits)**

Rate (*Circle one*)

Regular—$23 "Starving Artist"—$19.50 Child 12 & Under—$19.50

Foreign, *payable in US fund*s—$28

2

Name **Phone #** **E-mail**

Address **City** **State** **Zip (+ 4 digits)**

Rate (*Circle one*)

Regular—$23 "Starving Artist"—$19.50 Child 12 & Under—$19.50

Foreign, *payable in US fund*s—$28